John Hillaby

has been described as one of the world's greatest walkers. A tireless Yorkshireman who lives in London, he journeys alone and on foot, describing what he sees with fresh understanding. He strode the length of Britain, through Europe from the North Sea to the Mediterranean and across parts of boreal Canada and tropical Africa. Mr Hillaby is, moreover, a distinguished natural historian who for years wrote for the *Guardian* and *New York Times*.

The author has written seven highly popular books: *Journey to the Jade Sea*, *Journey through Britain*, *Journey through Europe*, *Journey through Love*, *Journey Home*, *John Hillaby's Yorkshire* and *John Hillaby's London*.

By John Hillaby

Journey to the Jade Sea
Journey through Britain
Journey through Europe
Journey through Love
Journey Home
John Hillaby's Yorkshire
John Hillaby's London

JOHN HILLABY

Journey to the Gods

Flamingo
An Imprint of HarperCollins*Publishers*

Flamingo
An Imprint of HarperCollins*Publishers*,
77–85 Fulham Palace Road,
Hammersmith, London W6 8JB

Published by Flamingo 1993
9 8 7 6 5 4 3 2 1

First published in Great Britain by
Constable & Co Ltd 1991

The lines from 'The Waste Land' by T. S. Eliot on page 214
are reprinted by permission of Faber and Faber

ISBN 0 586 08596 3

Set in Bembo

Printed in Great Britain by
HarperCollinsManufacturing Glasgow

Contents

With gratitude to the pathfinders:
Peter Levi, George Papadopoulos, Palinurus
and a score or more of
invaluable people in the mountains.

Introduction

During one blistering hot afternoon on the roof of the High Pindos, the central spine of Greece, we wondered, not for the first time, where on earth we could spend the night. We needed water, urgently, and also a reasonably flat patch of ground devoid of stones and prickly scrub. For hours and hours we had been trudging along narrow mountain ledges with occasional vertical drops on the sinister side. In the heat haze the distant peaks shimmered like a badly focused TV picture. We sweated. Our packs seemed to have redoubled in weight. When the sun began to sink, early, as it does in high places, we noticed that the gorge was spanned by power cables suspended on our side by an immense pylon. It stood on a promontory about sixty feet above us. Could I climb up to it and, if so, could I find a serpentine track well within the competence of Katie who, as the widow of a tea-planter on the slopes of Ceylon can clamber up almost anything?

G. all systems! I found not only something close to grass between the legs of the pylon but a springet of sparkling water. Two short blasts on the whistle we always carry meant I'd located the Arcadian equivalent of the Hilton. With a shove or two I helped her up to where, sheltered that night by the ventilated fly-sheet, we dined on dehydrated chicken soup, noodles and tinned octopus in tomato sauce,

7

commodities I hope never to taste again. Towards dawn – not far from half-past three – the sheet flapped in a warm wind and we heard harmonic howls which were either dogs on the loose, jackals or, possibly, wolves. About an hour later when we were thinking about packing up the sky was zipped open by a streak of lightning. A noise that resembled someone tearing a sheet of calico ended in a double explosion as if both barrels of a shotgun had been fired almost simultaneously. Situated as we were at the foot of one of the highest lightning conductors in the Pindos we had to get out, quick.

More howls before it began to rain with tropical violence. We scrambled down the scree and trudged on and on, until about midday we reached the hospitable hamlet of Marathos where we were looked after by the man who ran the place, 'Kaiser' Kapodistrio and his lonely friend Nico who lived in a world of his own making accompanied, occasionally, by a strange woman, a Vlach who 'had the sight'. An overnight stay there and we were off again. Long days of hard slog but, as used to be said of Africa, *semper aliquid novi*.

Newest of all were the ever-widening sights and insights we gained into the world of classical Greece, that is not merely majestic ruins of temples and monuments preserved in the aspic of tourism; by walking up through narrow passes and gazing down from summits we began to realize how ancient Athens and Delphi maintained their supremacy against the ferocious duplicity of Sparta. Likewise we discovered that the swamps of Boeotia must have been as important to The League north of the Gulf of Corinth as the walls and gates of Thebes.

Before we left we could not have had more erudite or entertaining instruction than the *Atlas of the Greek World* (1980) by Peter Levi and his translations of Pausanias, one paperback volume of which we carried throughout our whole venture. That gentle scholar Geoffrey Kirk fired our imaginations by much that he has written about Homer and the oral tradition. Apart from the poetic and distinctly theatrical intervention of the Olympian gods, is there any evidence whatever that there had ever been a Trojan War on the scale related in *The Iliad*? We set off with E. V. Rieu's translation and splendid commentaries on both that epic and *The Odyssey*, but were obliged to leave them behind in Delphi because of weight problems.

We read Patrick Leigh Fermor's intriguing accounts of the Vlachs or Wallachians before we struck up an enduring friendship with Nacu (John) Zdru. He still writes to us, regularly. When we returned to London my friend Tom Winnifrith, Chairman of the Joint School of Classics and Comparative Literature at the University of Warwick, an authority on these strange people, gave me abundant help by analysing their language and putting their arrival and departures into historical perspective.

As I shall relate, between the end of the Civil War and the beginning of the military dictatorship in Greece I had some brief employment in Athens and Delphi. On this journey we met the oldsters and the children of that terrible turmoil in the mountains where whole families fought against each other. We heard many stories. Nobody, in my opinion, has expressed them better than the late Kevin Andrews in *The Flight of Ikaros* (1959). I shall paraphrase one of them:

Sphakoanos was described as strong and careless, handsome, modest and generous. He had great style. In his belt he carried two pistols. One of them he called Maria and the other Eleni. One day he came into a village on Sunday at the hour when everyone was at the *Leitourgia*. He walked right into the church and called to the priest, 'Stop the Cherubic Hymn, *Dhespoti*!' He stepped up into the sanctuary himself, placed both

9

pistols on the Holy Table and began to pray. 'O *Panagia*, accept Maria and Eleni, and inspire all these thy servants to join ELAS this very minute or I'll blow their goddam brains out!'

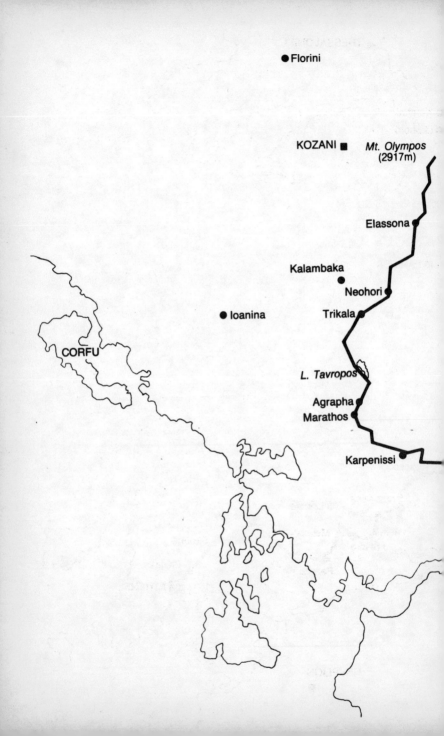

The *Flying Tortoise*

The railway station, the Ferrovia, is the back door, the tradesman's entrance to Venice. International tourists mostly fly to Marco Polo, the airport a dozen or more miles out of town, then they are driven along the narrow causeway across the swamps of the lagoon to the Piazzale Roma opposite the station, a square which, flanked by coaches and cars stacked away in enormous garages, is probably one of the ugliest in Europe. A pity, this. Even after three or four centuries of noble decay Venice is still very much of a piece entire. She has beaten the infernal combustion engine.

At high noon when bell-towers from the Giudecca to the Canale Grande proclaimed the Angelus, we sat at the foot of the Scalzi Bridge, arguing amicably whether to spend one more day in Venice or board the night express to Athens by way of Belgrade and Thessaloniki. Katie had a mind to take another look at the mosaics on the out-lying island of Torcello. I had just one thought, to push on, to start the long haul on foot from Attica to Mount Olympos on the fringe of Macedonia. I had been thinking about it for years.

After a snack we compromised by enquiring about the times of trains at the office in the station. They left each evening a little before six o'clock. 'Time to catch it tonight and see Torcello first,' I suggested, ever one for the best of all possible worlds.

'Not on,' said Katie. 'Venice isn't for rushing about. We haven't even packed. Let's spin for it. Heads we leave today; tails tomorrow.'

I'm a great believer in heads. For decisions on important matters the Roman legionaries spun a coin and called 'Heads or ships'. Those emblems must be of considerable antiquity. We were carrying a few Greek notes and coins. The current gold-coloured fifty-drach' piece bears the head of Homer on the obverse, and a high-pooped galley of the kind which might have been used by Odysseus on the other side.

I spun it, high. Blind Homer landed face downwards at the foot of a surprised porter. To compound disappointment on this party's part, an immense diesel engine slowly panted in, blowing out oily smoke-rings as if exhausted by her long run from Attica to the northernmost tip of the Adriatic. Whilst the passengers poured out and the cleaners squeezed in I looked at the monster with some curiosity. The logo on her flanks depicted a flying tortoise. Rather heavy symbolism, I thought – a view reinforced when I remembered that Pausanias tells a story about how an eagle, unable to smash the carapace of a tortoise, dropped it on the bald head of the dramatist Aeschylus. What for? Could it be that he had cast doubts on the immortality of mankind? Subsequent events were to lend some substance to that fanciful notion.

In the heat of an unseasonable sirocco we left the station and ambled back along the Lista di Spagna to the Canale di Cannaregio which runs through a nicely dilapidated native quarter free of tourists, including the old ghetto; thence by way of the Terra de S. Leonardo, the haunt of discriminating eaters with shallow pockets, and the Maddalena and the Ca'Rezzonico, where one may still see Browning's death-bed. A five-minute stroll along the Rio dei Gesuiti brings you out to the New Port where the gondoliers park their black swans within sight of the Island of the Dead.

I run over these names with affection since on our way to Greece on several occasions we've stayed in the same little place overlooking the Cannaregio. Venice is a place of coming and going. Those who stay there for any length of time go to escape from the twentieth century. Laurence Scarfe tells an engaging story of an eminent Venetian whose great passion in life used to be the London Underground. Seated in his lovely city he planned imaginary journeys from the Oval to Paddington.

I have little to say about Venetian glass; I don't like it; at least not the modern gimcrackery. But looking into the museum when the boat called at Murano, we marvelled at the nineteenth-century chandeliers, riots of coloured glass, firework displays suspended in mid-air, enormous examples of grandeur and folly. What must they have been like when flicker-lit by a hundred candles?

No stones of the cities of antiquity are quite so trite as those of Venice. They have been worn down, if not out, by centuries of tourism, adulation and literary scepticism. Distinguished visitors with a gift for surprising us object to feeling what they are supposed to feel in the presence of marvels. The 'dumpy Doges' Palace' exasperated Herbert Spencer to the point where he felt obliged to explain *how* it should have been built. What about St Mark's? He conceded it was a fine example of barbaric architecture. Towards the end of his life Ruskin, getting progressively grumpier, gave the impression that he would like to pull the place down. Three centuries earlier Montaigne was not so much impressed by the vaunted courtesans – 11,654 of them at that time – as by the police in their cocked hats and sabres, and the high cost of living: '*Les vivres sonts chers comme à Paris.*'

The languid island of Torcello is different. Instead of the mouldy, faintly putrescent smell of Venice the atmosphere is mildly marine, marvellously refreshing. Before the mid-season crowds swarm in one might stumble across a quiet garden set in the lagoon. With the need to reverse through acres and acres of reed-beds, the *vaporetto* inches up to a precarious landing-stage. Beyond lies a country lane hedged by hibiscus and tamarisk. On either side spread vineyards, orchards and fields of sweetcorn beset by poppies, long-stalked marguerites and sedge warblers. On that lane there is what looks like a village pub, but without a village since only a few buildings survive alongside the Basilica of Santa Maria Assunta and the double-domed Venetian-Byzantine style church of Santa Fosca.

The breath-taking glories of Maria Assunta, indeed of most if not all places which echo the remains of Venetian thraldom, are the mosaics of the vast barn-like Basilica. Here simplicity does all that the elaboration of St Mark's, St Peter's in Rome and many other less well-known cathedrals can never do. It is, says Scarfe, 'a church abandoned and all the better for it'. The city which used to be Torcello had gone before the cathedral plans were completed, and most of the marbles and porphyry, the inlays and incrustations, were shipped off to St Mark's.

The great mosaic of the Last Judgement on the west wall is the work of the twelfth and thirteenth centuries and is the only completed portion of what must have been a scheme to cover the whole of the interior. We are left to guess what the rest might have been like. Scarfe describes it as rising 'like a glittering cliff of precious stones and gold in an empty cave'. As if on ledges the figures are in layers, descending from Christ the Redeemer and the Heavenly Host down, far down, to the naked damned, writhing in an ossuary of shattered bones. In the central apse the lonely figure of the Virgin is curiously attenuated, almost flame-like, making it easier to understand why El Greco, the Cretan, put life into the timeless, the expressionless faces of Byzantine art he had known in his youth. Could it be that the glittering mosaics were inspired by iridescent fish scales, familiar to the restless inhabitants of a sea-kingdom?

Katie and I shouldn't have been there but for Homer, who foresaw that there were better things to do than rush about in trains. Nevertheless in the soft light of the evening I thought of the *Flying Tortoise* thundering towards Greece through the gorges of Slavonia.

The next afternoon we returned to the Ferrovia laden with rucksacks, food, wine and mineral water for two days of quiet window-gazing. We had booked first-class seats and hoped we'd have the compartment to ourselves. To our dismay, about half a minute before doors slammed and whistles shrieked, an elderly Austrian with a shaving brush attached to his deer-stalker clambered in, puffing and hauling up heavy zipped cases, baskets and two pieces of light artillery in canvas bags.

His name, he told us, was Fritzi, and, as if we hadn't guessed, he 'voss goin' untink'. Only one thing about our fellow-traveller really interested us and that was where he was getting off. Ljubljana he said which I reckoned about two or three hours away. During that time he talked, mostly about himself.

As the train began to ride rapidly over the sea we were absorbed in watching Venice sinking back into the lagoon. In the foreground mooring poles, power pylons and other life supports pierced the mud. Behind them the golden ochre, the pink and white of the campanile of St Mark's and the great green dome of S. Simon Piccolo lost definition in the general haze. Far away and scarcely visible were Murano, Burano and the small dot which I presumed was Torcello. *Clicketty-clank, clicketty-clonk.* We were being carried off, away to deeds of derring-do. The carnival was over, the brightness gone.

The door handle rattled. Passport control? No. An anxious lady from the next compartment broke in thinking we occupied the lavatory. Within half an hour we pulled into Trieste, a handsome city in its upper reaches or so I had read. Fritzi surprised us by saying that thanks largely to Maria Theresa it used to be Austria's most important seaport. He stood up, fumbled in a basket and produced a bottle of Bull's Blood. With much glass-clashing we toasted the Empress, mother of twelve children and, substantially, the founder of the Austro-Hungarian empire.

Good wine tends to evaporate. We carried something more than a litre of Chianti and food including Parma ham, mortadella, long rolls and various cheeses. Fritzi weighed in with thin slices of braised wild boar, some cognac and I forget what else. On the whole we did rather well. He told us how he had acquired the whiskers in his hat from the private parts (he patted his own) of an old wild boar. You had to hit them fast (*Abknallen*), he said, and to show how they did it with a Magnum .375 he snatched up one of our long rolls and put a shot clean through the head of a ticket inspector who just happened to be walking through the corridor.

In simple English and execrable German I tried to tell him how, from glimpses of wild boar (*Wildschwein*) in the Ardennes and the *Schwarzwald* I had got the impression they were not democratic animals. They felt far more at home under sporty *Herrenvolk* with land and trees and thickets and only limited time in which to shoot. They fled at the mere sound of the word Republic, the practical peasantry having no scruples whatever about exterminating pests which grub up their crops.

How much of this came over I don't know. It didn't really matter. We lifted our glasses to the *Wildschwein* everywhere, then to his family, to our families and to his success in the forests of Rosenbach north of Ljubljana. By the time we reached that station it took some time to decant the fellow on to the platform. Lest stone-throwing about intemperance sounds priggish, I'm obliged to admit that we had some argument about the basic mechanisms of pulling out our couchettes. And then we slept. We slept deep while the diesels thundered through the night, across the Sava Plain, towards Zagreb and Belgrade.

Came dawn, an ominous grey dawn with a rim of red light on the mountains above. We were on a single track in a deep gorge. I felt distinctly out of sorts but without disturbing Katie on the bunk above I couldn't get at the mineral water. I smelt coffee. Pulling on a shirt and a pair of pants I traced it to source, the steward at the end of the coach, talking to another passenger in what I took to be Serbo-Croat. They both smiled, greeted me in Greek and the steward asked if he could be of service.

Unable to recall the Greek for water I fell back on a smattering of German. '*Wassser, bitte. Kalt wasser und Kaffee.*'

No, I wasn't a German I assured him. *Engländer.* In the very essence of polyglot I did my best to explain that we were travelling to Athens to start a big journey, *grosse reise*, a *safari m'kubwa.* At those last two words in the kitchen Swahili to which I had become accustomed among natives during months in North Kenya he stared at me, open-eyed.

'You speak Kiswahili!'

I said yes, but I wasn't too good at it nowadays.

He grasped both my hands in warm greeting. '*Jambo, jambo sana!*' he said and laughed. Where had I picked it up? I told him. His name, he said, was Andriko. Unasked for, a generous brandy was poured into my coffee. It came out that like so many of his fellow-countrymen he'd spent fifteen years in a well paid but unpopular job in slaughter-houses in Nairobi and Kampala. He admitted that he'd come home with quite a lot of money.

What did his father do? He was a travelling shepherd.

'But from what country?' He smiled and shrugged his shoulders again. His parents came from many countries. North of Greece, I gathered, somewhere in the Balkans. I left it at that.

Silence for perhaps half a minute before Andriko said in a curiously slow and quiet voice, as if ashamed of his origins, '*Va him Vlachos.*' I wasn't too sure about the verb but that one word, that collective noun *Vlachos* rang like the first tremendous chime from Big Ben before the nine o'clock news.

Andriko and his family were Vlachs or Wallachians, descendants of many thousands of semi-nomadic Aromanians throughout the Balkans who used to migrate twice yearly between villages and their upland grazing-grounds. They speak a Latin-based language of their own which is akin to Romanian but as different from Greek as the Welsh language is from English. The very word 'Vlach' stems from the same root as Welsh and Walloon. It means foreigner or stranger.

At this point I am borrowing freely from the works of Patrick Leigh Fermor, especially *Roumeli* from which I learnt almost all I know about these extraordinary 'self-appointed Ishmaels' variously known as the Black Departers or the *Adespotoi*, those who refused to be mastered. Andriko looked at me anxiously. '*Sijui?*' he asked. Had I understood what he said?

I tried to assure him that it was a privilege to have talked to a Vlach. At this he seemed hugely pleased and reached for the brandy. I shook my head but said I'd like to take one back with a coffee for my wife.

Since Kiswahili in its crudest form is a kitchen language based, as somebody once put it, on the Ten Commandments and the Thirty-Nine Articles it would be tedious to translate the ins and outs of our elliptical talk together. Among other matters he wanted me to know that on the train, not far from our compartment, we should find the Big Chief of the Macedonian Vlachs. Nacu Zdru, he said, was his *koumbaros*, his greatly respected godfather. Perhaps I'd care to meet him? He spoke English since he lived for most of the year in California where he published a *gazetti*, bilingual news-sheet for emigrant Vlachs.

A pleasure, I said. On previous visits to Greece especially in the Pindos and mountains of Epirus we had seen the Black Departers, usually in clapped-out furniture vans, full of sheep, travelling at night. Paddy Leigh Fermor described them as 'Boojums to a man, who have perfected the art of Snark-like vanishing at the approach of trouble.'

When I was leaving, Andriko asked me if I would come back at eleven o'clock. Asked why, he glanced at his watch. 'There's trouble ahead,' he said, but didn't tell me what. At that his boss, the guard, wearing a cap decorated with a tattered strip of gilt, looked in. He had a worried expression and a large rail map. I left them to it.

All this took time to explain to a somewhat anxious Katie who said she'd begun to think I might have been left behind at Zagreb. Over breakfast we watched townships and villages with strange Slavonian names slip past; Baŏka Palanka, Vincovci and Sid Sabak. The Adriatic shoreline of Yugo-slavia is flanked by superb islands and coastal resorts, as I knew from boat trips from the Piraeus to Venice. But inland the country is thinly populated and looks wretchedly poor.

On a single track we swept into yet another gorge and the diesels throbbed as they hauled us out again into mountains as wild as any I've seen in Central Europe – dense forests of Caucasian pine and fir, waterfalls plunging down cliffs and rivers that looked treacherous. Good hunting country for our Austrian friend but not a place to bring up a family on a terraced holding hacked from a cliff. Somebody knocked on our corridor window, gently.

Enter M. Nacu Zdru from Kendrona in Macedonia. A well-dressed fellow, more than a shade overweight, who carried a large and expensive briefcase (Gucci). Speaking in the monotonic English of a Greek who had spent much time abroad, he seemed disinclined to tell us much about where he was born, or how or where he lived, except that it was on the coast just outside Los Angeles, but on one subject he exhibited the passionate dedication of a Jehovah's Witness and that was *Carti Vlaha-Engleza*, his news-sheets including bits of a dictionary and hundreds of simple phrases. He gave me a handful, over two dozen sheets. Two or three of them, I noticed, were sub-titled NEDREPTATI (Injustice). *Candu un poplu isi Chiari Limba, Poplu Atelu easti Mortu* – 'When a People loses its Ethnic Language that People has Died'.

Ever since Paddy Leigh Fermor whetted my curiosity about the Departers these were just what I had been looking for. Leigh Fermor breathes scholarship. He has lived in many parts of Greece; he can unravel their dialects and knows the Greeks themselves as well as any man can, but when he first tried to unravel the language and origins of the Vlachs or Wallachians more than thirty years ago even he was obliged to admit that almost everything he touched was hedged about with question marks.

As the route through Greece we had plotted would take us (we hoped) through Vlach country, it now seemed likely that we should be able to speak to them. Greeks tend to despise them, not least because of their clipped language. Later – when we had had time to learn quite a number of words and phrases – it seemed that there was much Latin, or neo-Latin, in their vocabulary. Perhaps I am romantically attached to the theory that they picked it up from Roman legionaries who guarded the passes through those worn out barriers of ancient mountains. Thus goodbye is *Oarâ-bunâ;* snow is *alba;* 'lemons are sour' is *acra easti limonia;* dog is *canili;* a goat *capra;* two goats *daua capri.* One of my favourite trees, the stream-shading alder, the *alnus* of Virgil, is *aluni* in the common talk of the *Adespotoi.*

After about an hour of somewhat one-sided conversation it became clear that Nacu was glad to meet someone interested in his fellow-countrymen. He rose to go. He had business in Belgrade and had other people to talk to before he got there.

'Just a minute,' I said. 'What's all this talk about big trouble ahead?'

'So Andriko told you?'

'Yes, but he didn't say what except that it was bad.'

Vlachs keep their cards close to their chests. '*Panagia,*' he said, invoking the name of the All-Holy Mother of God. 'It won't affect us.'

In one of my smatterings of Greek I hoped that his journey would be a good one. 'Goodbye,' I said, adding in his own language, '*Oarâ-bunâ.*'

An hour before high sun we moved down to Andriko's dispensary where he and two officials were looking through the window, anxiously. Monotonous countryside. Ten minutes passed. Almost nothing was said. Small drinks appeared. The roar of the diesels sank to a murmur. The sirens wailed. We were moving dead-slow. Andriko grabbed my arm and pointed. '*Tazana! Tazana!*' he said. 'Look! Look!'

Katie said afterwards that at first she thought we were passing a scrapyard where cars are crushed into blocks. Heavy cranes on the adjacent track were lifting up the tortured remains of coaches. Pieces of metal, wheels and pieces of wood fit only for a bonfire littered the ground. In the middle of the wreckage were two scarcely recognizable diesel engines. They had met, head on.

One was the prostrate skeleton of the *Flying Tortoise*, the train we didn't catch in Venice. The other, presumably from Athens, had half mounted her in a frightful caricature of copulation. Nacu reappeared. He shrugged his shoulders. Nobody could or would tell him what had happened or how many passengers had died.

I said we should almost certainly get the facts from the Greek newspapers. 'No you won't,' he said. 'At least, not from officials in *this* country.' Katie said firmly that we were getting off in Thessaloniki, 'and we're *not* getting back. No more trains. We'll take the bus down the Greek coast to Athens.'

Our diesels began to gather speed, slowly. We moved back to our empty apartment. There wasn't much to be said. But for the spin of a coin . . .

Down to the Start

What, until the advent of conceptual thought, had been a genuine oral tradition is now preserved in the aspic of tourism. For thousands of years there have been shrines to Zeus in many places as far apart as Dodona in Epirus to Mount Ida in Crete, but until we got off the train at Thessaloniki we knew of no temples on the heights of Mount Olympos, the ancestral home of the begetters of gods and heroes, and our eventual destination. So we were interested to learn from a week-old copy of *The Times* that on the very summit of the Olympian massif a team of archeologists under the distinguished Professor Dimitrios Pantermalis was hard at work excavating not only a temple there, but also several others lower down, and werè finding coins, inscriptions and the remains of animal sacrifices.

Thessaloniki, the second largest city in Greece, is rich in the remains of historic and prehistoric treasure. It was named after the half-sister of Alexander the Great, Aristotle's most famous pupil. Described as the 'lion-headed' man because 'his hair stood up from his forehead', he came near to conquering the whole of the known world.

Later, much later to preach in the synagogue of Thessaloniki, a Christian convert called Paul walked there along The Street called Straight, the *Via Egnatia* from Damascus and showed commendable restraint at the reception he received from his fellow-Jews when he remonstrated with them. Apparently the gospel of peace and goodwill towards all men had its ups and downs. Another convert, the Emperor Theodosius, slipped from grace by promptly ordering the massacre of 7,000 Thessalonians at a public festival in the Circus on the grounds that they had murdered one of his generals.

The story of all this and more, including the archaeological sites, the relics of outstanding battles with the weaponry and costumes of the combatants, are to be found in four well laid-out museums. I tried them all. In the absence of Professor Pantermalis I wanted to know what else had been found among the six peaks that marked the home of the Immortals. Their answers in French no better than my own were politely evasive: I might have been asking about the disposition of airfields on their Albanian and Bulgarian frontiers, which are very sensitive subjects anywhere in Greece.

A plain-speaking geologist from Massachusetts blew the gaff. With coloured felt-tips Jack (Jacques), on leave from MIT, was putting the final touches to a large-scale stratigraphic diagram of the whole Olympos range. We exchanged pleasantries and then he left me to admire his handiwork, saying he'd be back in five minutes as he'd promised to phone his girlfriend at ten o'clock.

The ground floor of the gods is more than a mountain, it's a fault-scarped massif riven by a huge gorge resembling the keystone of an enormous bridge which collapsed, leaving broken supports on either side. The serrations are what remains of the shared holiday homes of the landlord Zeus, Poseidon, Hades, Hestia called Vesta by the Romans, Demeter, Hera, wife and sister of the Gatherer of Clouds, and likeable Hephaestus, lame but with large lusty biceps, the super-craftsman, the smith-god revered among magicians and makers of ingenious things. Among his best pieces, his collection as they would call it nowadays, were the armour of Achilles, Harmonia's irresistible necklace and the sceptre of Agamemnon. So much for the heavenly crew.

Among competitive mountain climbers, *les conquérants de l'inutile* – those who seem to get their kicks from defying gravity – the peaks seen from left to right are Kalogeras, Antonios, Skolion, Skala, Mytikas (the throne of Zeus, the highest of all, 2,917 m) with Stefani, Toumba and Ilias only a few hundred metres below.

Jack came back, smiling. 'How's it going?' I asked.

'Sure thing,' he said. 'Maria's a Turkish Cypriot who wants to go to Paris. I'm teaching her French. It used to be my first language. Papa had a business in Quebec before we moved to Concord, and she's giving me lessons in Greek. What are you doing here?'

I told him and asked him the same question. 'Plate tectonics,' he answered. 'I'm here for three months hoping to get a doctorate out of the structure of the Olympos range.'

'Complicated?'

'Sure is. The trouble is there's next to no literature. I'm having to do my own field work. Now if only they'd found oil or even asbestos in them thar hills I'd be home and dry in a month. Almost the whole range is anomalous. The rocks on the top of the highest peaks are far older than those below them. It should be the other way round.'

To demonstrate what he meant he held his pen in a horizontal position and slowly tilted it to an angle of about forty-five degrees. 'That's what happened,' he said. 'A sort of see-saw effect. When the Aegean sank to its present level it shoved Olympos up in the air, far higher than it is today. My notion is that some of the uppermost rocks have been completely overturned.'

I steered the conversation round to the discovery of the temples. He said he'd heard about them but knew next to nothing about archaeology. I suggested that pilgrims and

29

shepherds had been walking over the ridge for thousands of years. Why hadn't anybody noticed the temples before now?

He pointed towards his coloured map. 'I can tell you what I know and also what I think. In addition to one huge fault between the major peaks the whole massif is unstable; it's riddled with fissures. Earthquakes are quite common. The range is trying to settle down. They tell me that two or three years ago there were spectacular cataracts in cracks where previously the peaks were covered in snow all the year round. The water brought down millions of tons of mud. Some of that mud, I think, had covered the graves which are now exposed. After all, it happened with ash at Pompeii. At phenomenal moments in time the treasures of the past can be "frozen".'

'But why are the archaeological people next door so cagey about saying what they've found?'

'Two reasons. You don't have to live in this city for very long to discover that the Alexandrian war isn't over as far as prestige and commercialism, especially tourism, are concerned. Thessaloniki and Athens are wildly envious of each other. They are under different administrations. I suspect the city here wanted to announce the news before the festival. The other reason is that archaeological sites are haunted by ghouls in the antique business. They prey on badly paid excavators who now and again slip a piece or two into their pockets.'

'About how far away is Athens from here?'

'Eight hours by bus.'

'Can you see the top peaks of Olympos from the highway?'

'Yes, if you travel soon after dawn when the east face is lit up. At this time of the year you're up against clouds and heat-haze after ten o'clock. The first bus leaves about seven. Slip the driver a couple of hundred drachs and ask him to stop or slow down at the turn-off to Litohoro, the nearest

village to the slopes.' Valuable information. We parted
warmly. Jack asked me to give him a ring if we reached the
peaks. By then, he said, he hoped to be sharing his pad with
Maria.

Katie had been spending an hour or two in Odos Mitro-
poleos and Tsimski where the best and most expensive shops
hugely enlarge covetousness. Before we retired to our
lodgings behind the old port we had booked seats in the
first Greek equivalent of a Greyhound bus to leave town
the next day. We had also walked the length of Vassileos
Konstandinou, the splendid promenade facing the Aegean,
that evening a wine-dark sea scarcely wrinkled by the
lightest of breezes.

We swung west an hour after dawn. From seats immediately behind the driver and his mate we looked down
on an enormous expanse of reedy rivers and fields of millet
and rice. All Greek buses are comfortable and the long-
distance runners are luxurious. As they overtake and weave
around smaller users of the four-lane highways their drivers
exude an air of ineffable confidence. They might be at the
helm of a cruise ship among a medley of bum-boats and
little freighters. Not for them, unfortunately, the cheerful
chatter, the camaraderie between passengers and crew as
we'd experienced it among the mountains of some of the
Greek islands.

In such places the transport of freight in labelled parcels,
baskets of fruit and vegetables, dressed chickens, hares and
on one occasion an excitable kid goat makes for amusement
all round, a running commentary on rural affairs. There is
a small charge for unaccompanied freight which is not
always adhered to. Katie recalled the solemn old man with
a sack of broad beans. Before he put them down between
the driver and the conductor he pulled out a handful, and

31

we were all given one pod each before he got off at the back without saying a word. My memory is of a frail soul in black who handed the driver a large basket of eggs together with a small bunch of violets for his dashboard, that area in which bus drivers take to the road under the protection of a picture of the Blessed Virgin, generally a statuette of Her Son on the cross, and rosaries surrounded by photographs of their wives and families.

We struck south and purred down to that shamble of narrow streets, the market town of Katerini, all business and huckstering. On both sides of the highway were new marquees, as might be the eve of Agincourt. Notices said 'Archaeological Sites'. In addition to the temples of Zeus the Greeks were unearthing what they believed to be the grave of Philip II of Macedon, father of the great Alexander. Interesting, certainly, but I felt tense. I had eyes only for the vast massif over my right shoulder. The horizons looked misty, tinged here and there with points of light as the crests caught the rising sun.

'How far is the *onomasti apopsi*?' – the famous vista – I asked the driver. 'Three kilometres,' he said. It felt like ten before he pulled up on the seaward side of the lane to Litohoro. Towering above the village the topmost crest of Olympos, the abode of the gods, broke through a veil of clouds. They slipped off her shoulders slowly, as if in a strip-tease act. Suddenly the light intensified to polished bronze and the highest mountain in Greece stood revealed in its majesty. The whole ridge remained coldly poised for perhaps two or three minutes, and then gradually faded from view. The sheer height of the escarpment looked spectacular and formidable. What were the chances of our being able to reach it? 'It's a cert,' said Katie, 'and now you'd better have a sandwich.'

During the long hours it took us to reach Athens classical names and places flickered past irrationally, like a video-tape spooled backwards. Ossa, you might say, was piled on Pelion – we slid round it before Olympos had slipped out of sight, an uninspiring mountain some miles to the south-east, with Turkish forts on nearby promontories. One of them, an American told us, is a resort for old voyeurs known nowadays as naturists. Pelion itself lay off our route.

We lunched at Lamia under a very untidy nest of storks and storklings on an old cartwheel, but saw little of the town as the bus stations of central Greece are built in un-accommodating places outside busy streets. Similarly about an hour later we'd hoped to get at least a glimpse of Thermopylae, literally the 'Hot Gates', but like Thebes, the home of that unruly fellow Oedipus, meaning Swollen Foot, the highway is miles away from what attracts the tourists. 'No matter,' said Katie, 'with any luck we shall be walking through the place next week.'

Aspects of Attica

Athens and its depressing suburbs have a resident population of two or three millions. In the Liossion area they swarm around the super-highway north. To the south-east the modern Panagi Tsaldari has been blasted through un-regenerate slums to the port of Piraeus. But in central Athens, that concentration of culture, there are highly superior districts sandwiched in between the great monuments of antiquity. By far the most elegant is the Kolonaki at the foot of Lycabettus, the Hill of the Wolves, that immense mound of pink-grey limestone nearly a thousand feet in height. Here are superb apartments, art galleries, antique dealers, luxury shops, pastry-cooks, restaurants and cafés with terraces where the cream of Athenian youth meets for a chat. Since the age of Pericles Athens has been known as the town of gossips.

At the top of a street so narrow, so steep, is a former embassy of a dozen rooms or more now tenanted by an old and most hospitable friend of ours whom, from his diplomatic associations, we call Our Man in Athens. A founder of the Eton College Archaeological Society, his interests after Christ Church, Oxford, first took him to the Middle East where he studied Arabic and Persian. Now retired from official appointments he writes intricate elegiac poetry.

After a day and a half in a train and eight hours in a bus lugging packs, we felt like ill-dressed pedlars in that well appointed suite. A bath and a change, and we rejoined our host on the vine-shaded terrace which almost encircles his floors. The panorama is superb. On all but the worst of days it stands above the smog. Nearby the eye is immediately caught by the Acropolis, lightly floodlit after dark amid points of light like a box of jewellery. To the east and north are the rims of the principal mountain peaks: Hymettus, the Pendeli and the massive bulk of Parnis.

Much had to be done before we tramped off into the hills and most of it had to do with maps and judicious enquiries about no-go military areas markedly unmarked on anything that could be bought or even looked at briefly. A few days elapsed before we discovered that large tracts of government forestry often screened political prisons patrolled by characters with automatic weaponry. Officials in the map dispensary near the Flea Market in Monastiraki sold us sheets (1:250,000) which were almost useless and quite inaccurate.

The business of the Hellenic Mountaineering and Skiing Federation was strictly limited to the heights used by those sports and how to get there by bus and funicular. What with one frustration after another, including a fruitless visit to the principal tourist office, we agreed to turn our backs on the town of gossips the next morning, and spent the rest of the day between the university and the luxury of the Kolonaki, largely for nostalgic reasons.

When peace broke out in 1945 the Greeks remained at each others' throats for almost another twenty years. Towards the end of totalitarian rule an international organization,* now part of the World Wildlife Fund (as it used to be called), decided to hold a conference in Athens with the hazy idea – which never came to anything – of turning

* *The IUCN, International Union for Conservation.*

Delphi, the navel, the *omphalos* of the classical world, into a permanent cultural centre with the emphasis on studying ecology throughout the world. As European science correspondent for the *New York Times* I volunteered to act as honorary Press and Information Officer to the whole affair, and soon wished I had stuck to my own business.

Events became mildly chaotic from the start. At eleven o'clock on the first night a German delegate from the Bundesrepublik, who had been billeted in Athens in 1943, beat on the front door of the home of my Greek liaison officer, Peter Petriades, a young professor of biology. With insensitivity almost beyond comprehension, the German wanted to show his wife where he had acted as *führer*. As he'd been implicated in atrocities which resulted in the death of a member of Peter's family it was not surprising that he was hit on the nose, hard. Apparently he didn't know whose home he'd partly ransacked when he and the occupying force fled. This caused a marked degree of tension among some noteworthy delegates.

We had mustered 300, most of them reckoned to be their country's leading ecologists, from twenty nations ranging from the United States to China, which was represented by the diminutive figure of Dr Te-Chee Poo and his wife. At a banquet in the Grande Bretagne hotel on the second night a group of Russians were unduly serious and uncommunicative until they discovered that ouzo from Lesbos was stronger and more palatable than their best vodka. Before the evening was over two of them had to be restrained by the management from Cossack dancing and throwing crystal goblets on the chairman's table.

During the opening session when our beribboned president and his inner council were engaged in cascades of French rhetoric, I sat as lonely as a cloud in a back room of the main university building, surrounded by foot-high piles of translations of the principal papers. About a dozen pressmen wandered in, led by two shrewd characters from Reuters and UPI. In English and imperfect French I tried to sell the ecological idea of a prosperous world fit to live in and good to look at.

Had the threat of extinction to the Javan rhinoceros, the Asiatic lion and the Crested coot anything to do with hungry nations, I was asked. I managed to fend that one off, but slipped up badly by mentioning the idea of a cultural centre in Delphi. That brought me head up against the return of the Elgin Marbles: what did Britain intend to do about them? Had King Paul approached Harold Macmillan, I was asked. I simply didn't know and yearned for the arrival of Peter Petriades. He was cooling off somewhere or other, talking to his Greek colleagues.

'You should put that question to the British cultural attaché,' said an attractive silvery-haired woman who had walked in unnoticed by me but not the local press. Knowing I knew precious little about Greek politics after the Civil War, Madame Iphigenia, wife of a general and doyenne of our local Ladies' Committee, effectively took over the briefing by translating and making suggestions, without in any way impairing my slender authority. I discovered afterwards that she and her husband, a former Foreign Minister, lived in a château above the Gulf with an apartment in Kolonaki. They belonged to that rich Athenian set who could say of almost everybody in a succession of cabinets: '*Vous savez, mon cher, il est un de mes cousins.*' On that morning, putting stuff across to the press and radio, and thereafter socially, I owed a great deal to her. 'Phone this number,' she would say, handing me her card, 'and give Gregor my compliments.' It was the Minister of Communications, a tyrant.

The next day Peter, with his knuckles bandaged, and three other speakers gave short papers during a plenary session on the subject of erosion, a dramatic occasion which brought us more publicity than anything else that week. After a sweltering hot morning a cold wind started to blow from the north. It became curiously dark. Lightning flickered over the city. After one gunshot-like crash of thunder our lights went out. The caretaker, I knew, lived nearby and I went out to look for him. All traffic had come to a standstill. The road-surface of Venizelos looked steamy under a rainstorm of tropical violence. The gutters were blocked with brownish silt. The caretaker said it was the *meltemi* and hurried back to start the emergency generators. I scooped up a few spoonsful of the slush in my handkerchief and went back to the lecture theatre.

A dull but diligent fellow from the Peabody Museum at Yale was droning on about siltation problems in the storage dams of South Dakota. I caught Peter's eye, beckoned to him and showed him what I'd brought back. He rubbed some grains between his fingers, smelt it and said: 'That's *just* what we want. The *meltemi* is the wind that's helping to destroy Greece.' Within minutes he'd brought back a microscope and a projector from his laboratory.

His extempore address on 'The Fate of Arcadia' brought the press and radio back within an hour. Sketching rapidly with chalk on a blackboard, he showed how the furious wind had picked up the sun-baked soil of the north and hurled it down into Attica, where clouds of dust sparked off electric storms. That's why, he explained, their mountain tops were bare and the eastern Mediterranean was rich in humus which became fish food. 'Overgraze the land and think only of this year's crop and not what your children will inherit, and you'll be left with what you'll see on tomorrow's tour of Mount Parnassos – bare mountains. That's the message,' he said.

I sat up until midnight, answering telephone calls from the radio, the press and news agencies. It became front page news in several national newspapers.

Verbal snapshots of Greece flicker in and out of the diaries which have accompanied me since I first began to travel abroad. There was Anastasia, our guide during regular bus tours of the city. Her knowledge was as remarkable as the laconic way in which she put it across. She stood with her back to the driver whilst we cruised round the Kendriki Agora. 'On the left', she said through the microphone, 'there is a statue attributed perhaps wrongly to Praxiteles and on the right there is an accident.'

In the company of Mme Iphigenia and the wives of some delegates we walked round Syntagma Square. Assuming from her faultless accent that she was English, a gravel-voiced American woman, a stranger, asked her some questions about the palace guards, the *evzones* in their distinctive kilt and pom-pom shoes who perform a sort of military ballet. She answered her courteously and in some detail. The American stared at her hair. 'Say!' she said in admiration. 'How d'ya get a hairdo like that in this dump?' Mme Iphigenia smiled. 'At Christian's in the Kolonaki,' she said. 'Perhaps you'd care to give them my card?'

Until I mentioned the incident to my friend Peter I couldn't understand why one of the best-known socialites in the city hadn't betrayed at least a touch of asperity in replying to a downright rude woman. 'Because she's a diplomat and the wife and daughter of a diplomat,' he said. 'Her husband Stephanos, a nephew of King Paul, goes shooting with the King. To have acted otherwise would have gone against the ritualism attached to our national conception of *philotomo* which is stronger than the Oriental notion of "face". We Greeks are a kindly people at heart. But kindliness doesn't neutralize an occasional streak of ferocity. The same could be said for your Irish and a helluva lot of those bloody Germans.'

Keeping *philotomo* in mind it became possible to speak more intimately to my graceful companion. Apart from her social obligations, how did she spend her time, I asked her. '*Mon cher*,' she said, 'in a dozen different ways. Mostly gossiping and taking short walks with nice young men.' Stephanos, I learnt later, had similar preoccupations with an unquestionable emphasis on the latter pursuit, a Greek frailty to which were added the opportunities of a former Foreign Minister.

Towards the end of our conference Iphigenia invited me to dine with them at their villa overlooking the Gulf of Corinth. Three kings had stayed there. I can't recall what sumptuosity was laid out, but there was one notable lapse from grace on this party's part. Before the fish Stephanos asked what wine I fancied and I said that I had developed a taste for retsina. A moment's silence ensued before he said no doubt they could find some, suggesting it was normally tippled by his chauffeur. Dinner over and brandy served, Madame took my hand and the three of us stood together on their terrace overlooking the Gulf freckled with the lights of shipping. As I stood between them in the velvety dark, close, I could scarcely distinguish my hosts. To my surprise a hand lightly stroked my backside. I hadn't realized she thought that much about me. Alas, the hand was not hers.

Nearly forty years later Katie and I wandered up through the Kolonaki, past the bell-booming church of St George the Martyr and through a path alongside the funicular to the summit of the Hill of Wolves. When Lycabettus was more remote from the walled town of gossips than Hampstead Heath is from Piccadilly Circus, Pausanias tells us that the wolves constantly menaced shepherds and their flocks. Old soldiers with bows were hired to keep them at bay. Today the track is bounded by vicious cactus and Caucasian pines. We talked about how we should weave through the labyrinth of Liossion. Tomorrow and tomorrow . . .

Apart from the effluent traffic at six o'clock in the morning on even the back roads out of town, the day dawned like any other. Unfortunately we'd overlooked the fact that 1 May would be a national holiday when gregarious Greeks take to the country in their family cars and drive nose to tail, like migratory lemmings, intent on a meal of roast lamb in the open air.

Our reason for starting walks from the centre of cities instead of taking some form of transport to their outermost suburbs is immoderate pride in the phrase 'journey on foot'. In Athens we were obliged to pick our way through the run-down area of the Patissia. Even in its heyday – that is, what Osbert Lancaster called the 'early Compton Mackenzie' period – it could never have been rated above the shabby-genteel, whilst after the German Occupation it became the stamping-ground of the cheaper sort of whores and the starting-place for all the more violent Communist demonstrations.

Osbert Lancaster's explanation for what happened in the Patissia and, indeed, in the long monotonous streets around the National Archaeological Museum is 'a remarkable demonstration of that rugged individualism which makes the Greek planners' lot so hard'. Apparently it had been intended by the city fathers that the future development of Athens should be an orderly southward expansion, eventually linking the city with the Piraeus, and plans to that effect had been drawn up. However, before they could be carried out a shrewd Athenian of that period, the grandfather of the eminent publicist, George 'Colossus' Katsimbalis, operating along lines exactly opposed to those which have been so successfully pursued by land speculators in our own country, bought up all the land he could lay his hands on to the north of the town. As he had anticipated, the moment it was suggested to the Athenian public by the planners that they should dwell to the south, they rushed out and bought building sites in exactly the opposite direction, and the psychologist's fortune was made.

By many a turn and twist to avoid the main roads we trudged through as rich a variety of contrasts as ever you can find on either side of London's north-western highway, the Finchley Road.

Between Iraklion Street and Philadelphia there are a few run-down mansions that smack of the poorer Bavarian relatives of the Greek King Otto, but the peeling white stucco looks leprous, often carbonized by the fumes from the repair shops for clapped-out trucks and motor-bikes on the ground floor. Withered relics of a vine or bougainvillaea are sole witnesses to former greatness.

The buildings to the north tend to become more and more commercial, relieved only by brave little houses with cascades of pendulous geraniums rooted in white-painted petrol cans. A feature of the domestic architecture is that few blocks of small apartments are completely roofed over: they are topped by tubular scaffolding, the framework of yet another floor for which there are taxation concessions. A common pattern of development is for cousin Spiros to return from fifteen years' exile in Australia, Germany or the States with more money than he has ever earned before. His biggest problem is to buy land in a country where the strict laws of inheritance may have ensured continuity of tenure for a hundred years or more. This sometimes results in an elderly grandmother with the tenacity of a hermit crab occupying two rooms in a building part of which has been twice pulled down and rebuilt. But once Spiros has acquired his plot he starts to build two floors, one for himself and his family with a lodger or tenant upstairs whose rent pays for more development.

The sight one day of a truly weird machine resembling

an enormous vacuum cleaner that roars as it vomits liquid concrete between wooden moulds on the third apartment-to-be shows the whole neighbourhood that the prodigal son is both physically and metaphorically on the way up. Spiros has another financial card up his sleeve before he fulfils his dream of retiring to lead the life of Larry on the island of Mykonos where his grandmother's health and estate management are anxiously watched by her grandchildren. Within a month of getting his first job in, let us say, Chicago Spiros started to subscribe to Illinois Mutual from which a pension, small by US standards, is worth a great deal more when transferred into drachmas.

Beyond the small circle of the exceptionally rich, land for building purposes in Greece is not bought for the isolation it affords. Sociability is the rule. The majority of Greeks who like to live high in the physical sense of the word are not so much concerned about who might overlook their activities as consumed by insatiable curiosity about the goings-on of their neighbours.

We trudged on and swung left down a promising side street only to find ourselves confronted by a bewildering complex which included the super-highway to Thessaloniki, a railway line and three other roads one of which led up into the heights of Mount Parnis, mostly for the winter ski-runs. Lost in Liossion after only two hours' walking, we thrashed about until we met a genial old fellow leading a donkey who, when we managed to make it clear that we were making for Kamatero at the foot of the hills, guided us through the cat's cradle of stone and tar. The walls of ruined warehouses still bore the almost obliterated graffiti of bygone battles in the streets. The ominous word ΘΑΝΑΤΟΣ (death) and the symbol of a man swinging from a gibbet had been sprayed on the blue crown of the monarchists. ΔΕΜΟΚΡΑΤΙΑ (democracy) was almost self-explanatory, likewise KKE and a red hammer and sickle but

I doubt whether we could have worked out ΖΗΤΟ ΣΤΑΛΙΝ if our guide hadn't grinned, clenched his fist and said, 'Stalin'.

We shook hands, warmly, and parted on the extension of Liossion Street, the road to Kamatero. '*Kalo taxidi,*' he said – may your journey be a good one – but he shook his head slowly as he tested the weight of our rucksacks. Already we knew they were too heavy.

The Athenians were taking to the hills. By ten o'clock the stream of cars had risen to a cataract. Family cars raced past us in scores, some of them trailing multi-coloured ribbons, their occupants hooting and waving. The bonnets of most of the vehicles were decorated with bunches of yellow flowers which at first I took to be gorse but from a stationary minibus with an impressive geyser hissing from its radiator I recognized broom, *Planta genista*, symbol of our kings from Henry II to Richard III, a plant of many virtues, medicinal, magical, amorous and domestic since the tough stems can be used for sweeping up. The plant is associated with lovers, witchcraft and veniality. It relieves the bladder and promotes drowsiness, a state in which much can be accomplished. A medieval poet wrote:

> *Tell me, O being in the broom,*
> *Teach me what to do*
> *That my husband*
> *Love me true.*

The holidaymakers were intent on whooping it up. We had some difficulty in dodging them and when we got to Kamatero, the first village, we disliked the place from the start. The sole tavern-keeper with an open door and sounds of music within said, with scant regard for logic, that it was closed. Probably in our haste to get away from the place we took a wrong turning with confidence. Voltaire says that doubt is not a pleasant condition, but over-certainty is an impossible one.

The rural road wriggled about like a wounded snake and when from a rocky knoll we took our bearings, we saw we need not rely on the compass. Far away to the west there appeared the Gulf of Corinth. In scrubby country where all mounds look much alike we were close to ninety degrees off course. We sighed, turned round slowly and started a cross-country diagonal, over ditches, through groves of ancient olives, around fields of withered corn and the terraced ruins of vineyards. No paths worth the name. That zealous fell-walker, Alfred Wainwright, said that path-finding in cultivated country is more prone to error and exasperation than among desolate mountains anywhere. The air felt both hot and moist. You could push it with your hand. We were climbing fairly steeply. One recompense for tackling parallel ridges is that you can hope for encouragement on the crest above. Maybe another false crest or a glimpse of the promised land.

The sudden appearance of a lurcher under the ruins of a cart gave cause for apprehension: an uncommonly large and hairy dog which did nothing except slowly sink to the ground with ears lowered and gaze fixed, I imagined, on my bare ankles. It didn't bark, another bad sign. Edward Lear, in his walk through southern Greece a century ago, hired unemployed men with *kourbachi*, horsehide whips to beat off vagrant hounds, the descendants, in his opinion, of the Spartan dogs of war. His party repelled attacks several times and he relates how an ancient shepherd 'with a face like a door-knocker' nearly suffered the fate of Actaeon when, at the sound of Lear's gunshot, a pack of six turned round and fell on the man who had been urging them on.

The lurcher, if such it was, disappeared during our elaborate detour but turned up again on the next ridge, lying on its back and wriggling, an old bitch in need of a little affection. With more confidence than I had, Katie scratched it between the ears and, with an opportunity for taking off our packs, we gave it some biscuits. We set off again, trying to make it plain to the animal that we'd had enough of it.

The last ridge disclosed first the top of a thunderhead of Zeus, the Gatherer of Clouds, an almighty anvil-shaped mass of cumulo-nimbus with, partly obscured below, the blue-grey summits of the Parnis range beset by racing cloud shadows. As we quickened step down a steep path a ribbon-shaped village appeared from which arose curious plumes of smoke as if a tribe of red-men were sending out urgent signals.

At three o'clock in the afternoon we reached Phyle where whole flocks of lambs were being sacrificed and spit-roasted. Scores of trippers had settled on the village. In addition to two overcrowded tavernas there were family parties and community parties with roasts on glowing beds of charcoal from which arose plumes of thyme-scented smoke which united in one pale blue cloud above the defile. We had relied on being able to order a meal but waiters scurrying between tables made it clear that they were booked up for at least two hours.

'Good day, friends. What's the problem?'

Despina had the compassionate, the almost ethereal face of a young girl who had learnt to live with a deformity, a fearfully twisted leg – a car accident, she told us. A librarian in Melbourne, she had come back to Thebes, her birthplace, on her first visit since she had left at the age of eighteen to marry an Australian doctor. Next to her sat Granny, an old lady with brown, deeply lined features, unquenchable curiosity and wit although she scarcely spoke more than a few words of English. Despina translated. She called a waiter with an order for two more portions to be added to their own and there began the first of two memorable encounters on our first day out.

In addition to the Greek's passion for company is a way of putting wholly uninhibited questions to strangers to which we had become accustomed in our wanderings around the Peloponnese and the islands. One's immediate and future business, one's age, health, income, marital status and views about the Greek way of life, are all matters in which they take a burning and perfectly genuine interest and on which deliberately to withhold information would be considered churlish. Whether the grand-daughter would have been equally forthright is difficult to say.

After we had gone over the nuts and bolts of our intentions, Granny abruptly asked *why*?

'Curiosity,' I said to Despina.

It took two sentences to interpret that one word. Sensing we were rather enjoying the quiz-game, our interpreter said: 'Granny wants to know who pays you.'

'Books and articles,' I said.

Granny turned the matter over as she slowly dissected a titbit from the charred shoulders of the lamb. Eventually, wiping her mouth with a tired carnation which had fallen to the table, she asked how old I was. I told her. She nodded, apparently satisfied and munched away before saying, in translation: 'You are fortunate. You will have a good journey. We Greeks respect old men.'

A silence in which I poured another round of light Demestica, from which Despina refrained since she intended to drive Granny home. A little matter of property was involved. Opening her eyes as if from profound thought, the old lady asked whether my wife always wore jeans. I said no, she always carried a formal dress but we had walked from Athens that morning and intended to spend the night in a tent. Translating slowly as if dissociating herself from the comment, Despina replied: 'She says, "Good. In a skirt, the Mother of God (*Panagia*) will always protect her. Especially in the mountains." ' She added something else in Greek which I took to be a mild reproof. 'My family', Despina explained, 'are rather old-fashioned Boeotians. They have a reputation for kindliness but don't take to modern ways. Hard-working but slow. Perhaps it's the air over the plains, which you'll find is heavy and without movement. Good for growing vegetables.'

Not for the first time that day we had some difficulty in refusing an offer of a lift up into the hills. It was difficult to explain briefly and graciously the pride we took in trying to walk every foot of the way. If up into the hills, why not on to Thebes, or even further? It can't have been easy to translate to the old lady who asked, predictably, why we couldn't enjoy ourselves in one of the comfortable buses lined up to ferry the holidaymakers home.

Attempts at a reasonable answer were cut short by a muscular and bare-chested Greek youth who wove his way somewhat unsteadily to our table since, as I understood it, he knew our elderly Boeotian friend. He went through the pleasant rituals of touching his forehead and bowing to all of us. Despina said: 'He wants to know if you'd accept a drink from a lover of the British people and might he, please, try to lift your huge pack?' He meant both packs. Machismo.

He bowed again, took a deep breath and picked up one in each hand in the manner of a Japanese wrestler poised for the first grapple. He fell, or at least he staggered backwards where he bumped his bottom against the next table and knocked over two or three glasses of wine. He lowered our packs and looked aghast at the dripping surface.

They each said something, loudly. A confrontation? The

man at the table stood up, put his arms round the other's shoulders and kissed him on both cheeks. What had he said? 'He has assured him that every action has its charm,' said Despina. And the young man? 'He will be indebted to him for life. The difference', she added dryly, 'between a man from Athens and a man from Thebes.'

Our young friend had studied Greek history, and before we parted she told us that for ancient Attica, Phyle was of tremendous importance. It used to be the central pass of the great wall of the Parnis range, forming a natural and easily defensible frontier against their enemies, the Boeotians. The other passes were Eleftherae to the west and Dekelea to the east. The latter gained fearful notoriety when it was betrayed to the Spartans by Alcibiades, the pupil and intimate friend of Socrates. Fearful lest they should also lose the Phyle pass, the Athenians sought divine help. During thundery weather they posted augurs on the towers above the gorge who at the first flash of lightning were instructed to send messengers to Delphi to make suitable sacrifices to the Lord of Storms. 'They would have been busy this evening,' Despina said, looking out at the ominous sky. 'Are you sure you wouldn't like a lift?'

Lightning flickered as we climbed up the Gorge of the Virgin, the Panagia Kliston, topped by a monastery – not in forks or bright sparklets but dully as might be from a faulty fluorescent tube. The cars of a few holidaymakers growled down in low gear. We could hear them coming from somewhere in the gloom above. Impossible to guess how high we were and how long it would take to reach a recommended tavern near the summit, since contours on Greek maps are haphazard and never disfigured by numbers. I had reckoned on a walk of five or six miles and assumed that a gorge was a gorge and not a staircase of twisting roads.

An hour passed. More heavily buttressed bends in the narrow road of the kind known in France as *lancettes*. In vain I combed the air for evidence of life, the sight of a bat or the call of a bird. We heard only the sound of our feet on the gritty surface.

We discussed the questions that had been put to us and I wondered why I hadn't given a straight answer to the one about being burdened like Balaam's ass. The answer surely was that with a tent on our backs we could stop for the night anywhere and in any sort of weather. Or could we? As we were to discover often in the ensuing weeks, even the toughest groundsheet affords no protection against the prickly scrub of the Mediterranean. It left no alternative but the road and the hazards of wheeled traffic.

Another hour passed. From somewhere on the almost flat and almost parallel road just above came the increasingly loud noise of falling water until, after swinging round the next bend, we peered over the parapet of a cataract that fell thirty or forty feet before plunging into a hidden defile: overhanging trees and protrusive boulders amid a tangle of thorny vegetation marked its visible course. Nowhere could we have placed our bedding down there.

The mist thinned, two more *lancettes* appeared above our heads and gradually we came out into groves of juniper and Cephalonian pine. We had emerged from the top of a thin bank of cloud. A signpost pointed on the one side to the Monastery of the Virgin and on the other to Thebes. Not very helpful. The lightning flickered again. Under such circumstances, we are told, Socrates accepted the fatal cup.

Few signs could have been more welcome than a board nailed to a tree which pointed up a heavily churned-up dirt track and simply said *Taverna 100m*. We walked down to a clearing and found a huge wooden shed in which four men staggered about, washing trestle tables and piling them up around a garbage-littered floor scavenged by a host of quarrelsome cats. Brothers Megaros were so tired they didn't even seem surprised to see two rather elderly English walkers appear out of the storm. They were almost totally exhausted after serving, one of them told us, more than 1,000 hungry visitors that day. At the mention of drink – we felt we'd earned a strong one – and perhaps a little food, the youngest of them clicked his tongue, closed his eyes, tilted back his head and slowly lifted up his arms, palms uppermost, which requires no explanation from the Romanian border to the Peloponnese. Speaking very basic Greek, Katie pointed to two empty chairs and a table and asked if we might sit down for a little while as we had walked a long way. That seemed to be all right, and as if walking in his sleep the man turned round and carried on sweeping.

Silence on our part. Bats snapped up huge moths around the butane lamps. With no enthusiasm I thought of our emergency supplies: instant coffee, packets of dehydrated food and vitaminized fudge, the latter particularly useful for making friends with dogs of uncertain temper.

Katie said this wasn't the time to keep going on about the stiff one – I tend to go on about all sorts of things – but just to be a little patient until they'd caught up with things. She might have been overheard. The banging and clattering ceased. Laughter, snatches of song and a short burst of recorded music. We felt abandoned, but not for long. They all came over. One of them put a woven shawl around Katie's shoulders, another a basket of bread on the table whilst the third carried plates of cold meat. It looked as if we were being offered a laid-aside portion of their own meal.

They over-poured glasses of warmish red wine, a strong local vintage which was more than acceptable, and we invited them to share it.

The cup had gone round three or four times before a

flash of pale-blue light and the crash of what could have been a shot from a twenty-five pounder echoed from the roof of Karampola. Huge spots of rain. Clearly the time had come to leave. Where could we sleep? On padded chairs in the dining-room, they suggested. Then on the grass of their car-park, they said, obviously puzzled.

I could do nothing about the reckoning which in drachmas came to the equivalent of about two pounds, and amid embraces all round we left to put up our tent in the pouring dark just out of sight of their windows.

Whilst shoving the telescopic ribs of our hemisphere into seams below the outer fly sheet we got pretty wet, but once that's done there are physically no strings to it and we can crawl into our igloo as if under the shell of a tortoise. Then we can peg down the wafer-thin inner fly and groundsheet all in one, in relative comfort, zip our sleeping-bags together and arrange all our bits and pieces around us.

With half a dozen pegs between her teeth Katie muttered: 'Why on earth couldn't we have stayed under their roof?'

'The party showed signs of going on for another two hours,' I said. 'We can probably be up and away before seven o'clock. There's nothing better than independence.'

'With or without water?' she asked quietly, thinking about our dehydrated breakfast.

The hiss of rain subsided. Within twenty minutes it had stopped. Feeling no end of a fool I pulled out the canvas water-bag and returned to the kitchen where they were lolling back with their legs on a table looking rather the worse for wear. Water? Hadn't we seen the tap in their car-park? But water needed to be flavoured – and they pushed a tin mug of Metaxas into my hand.

We sipped it in the warm dark of the tent where I found Katie looking out through the unzipped outer fly. Somewhere nearby a frog belched, to be answered almost immediately by cork-popping noises and trills in different keys by many others. As we slipped off to sleep the chorus rose and fell, making about as much sense to our ears as a flute concerto by Schoenberg.

Two against Thebes

We opened our eyes early, or at least one of us did. It needed a kiss on the shoulder and a gentle shove lower down to bring Katie back from dreams of West Hampstead to the realities of outermost Attica. 'Wha' time's it?' she asked, and on hearing that she had lost near half a day in sleep – wholly untrue – she woke with what alacrity could be expected.

Towels were exchanged as we shivered under the car-park tap; plastic mugs were brought out, the butane burner roared. Nescafé spiked with the last thimbleful of Metaxas gave slight heart for a shared packet of dehydrated beef and vegetables and we started to pull our portable igloo to portable size.

Even with the latest equipment this is a dispiriting exercise on a wet morning. Whilst shaking ice-cold droplets from the outer fly we decided against an idea that it was warm enough in Greece to allow us to leave the inner skin on the doorstep of our generous hosts. We rammed down our possessions into gaping rucksacks, ensuring all the heavy stuff sat on our shoulders and so on.

Unquestionably overloaded, we wondered whether to sacrifice our heavily annotated copy of Pausanias, the Michelin Guide or an illustrated work on the flowers of Greece, but all these were trivial compared with the weight of the Pentax and its zoom lenses, the spare tin of liquid gas

and an all-purpose skinning-knife I had carried from
Yorkshire to North Kenya. In the end we took them all
along.

The last look round. No litter, no combined tin-opener
and corkscrew left in the rank grass. And then, pause, I
gripped Katie's pack under the shoulder straps, lifted it on
to my right shoulder and hooked it over her upheld arms.
It felt dreadfully heavy, the curse of Atlas. Mine too, but
with all stowed away we set off for another long haul.

The small road from the taverna lapsed into a well-trodden
track bordered with shy flowers in the ditches, especially
wild orchids: that handsome commoner, the Butterfly
orchid with large pinkish bracts and her cousin with her
green wings in a loose spike, and *Dactylorches*, too, with
flowers graded from violet to the colour of Cornish butter.
Here seemed all we had been promised for high Attica in
the season of flowers.

The path from the road, unmapped of course on the
government sheet, narrowed and then suddenly disappeared.
Not in a flurry of options or because of some obstruction
but peremptorily, as if banished by state decree. Only a small
pile of stones and the ruins of a truck marked its sudden
abdication. This left us puzzled and indignant. By what
authority had the wayleave, fortified by the local knowledge
of our hosts, been withdrawn? Apparently we had crossed
the unmarked boundary between the prefectures of Attica
and Boeotia, the first one rich and the other relatively poor.
In my imagination I can now see the leading citizens of
Athens and Thebes at last agreeing on a piece of infertile
land on which nobody was prepared to settle, a rocky place,
deficient in calcium and phosphorus, fit only for some
Boeotian Esau.

Ahead lay a waste of rock and mica-glinting sand thickly-
populated by clumps of *Quercus coccinea*, the foot-tripping
scrub oak, only ankle high but seemingly devil-deep. Here

and there were ghostly drifts of asphodel which, inexplicably, is reputed to flourish in the Elysian fields, a stiff unlovable lily which according to Anthony Huxley is often a sign of derelict ungrazed ground. The plant is not usually eaten by animals. Its tubers, rich in starch, are used to make glue for shoemakers and book-binders. Huxley notes that the flowers of two sorts, white and yellow, 'are sometimes planted around graves because the roots were thought to nourish the spirits of the dead'. Understandable. Our daffodil is a corruption of the ancient Greek word associated with gloom and glue.

Between eight o'clock and high sun we saw not a single soul among those lightly clothed ridges of red earth with tares and thorns that put us in mind of illustrations of the biblical wilderness, but we gained what comfort we could from the fact that our march north-west by north was matched by a line of huge pylons which, we assumed, were carrying Athenian power to Thebes. Katie as usual endured the harsh landscape with better grace than I did, and when the arid plants and a few birds, mostly Crested larks and squeaky creatures like small partridges, probably quail, failed to hold our attention for long, we exercised our imagination. I discovered a Lost City. Not perhaps a city, scarcely a village with the ruins of walls and gates almost covered with prickly oak and blanched vines, and I'm not sure it was lost, but we told ourselves that it might have been the last defence line of ancient Boeotians against their traditional enemies, the Plataeans who lived to the north of the Gulf of Corinth.

Because of the ridge-and-furrow nature of the terrain we couldn't see the pylons from the hollows but from the crests they appeared to be slipping out of sight. Clearly we were throwing away altitude hard gained the previous night, and were glad of it. Patches of corn appeared. Hardly worth harvesting, I should have thought, since in places the meagre crop could scarcely be seen for spikes of purple gladiolus and acrid euphorbia bloated with poisonous sap. From the top of one steep crest we looked down on an extensive marsh with pools that winked like watery eyes. Here, surely, were the outliers of those famous Boeotian swamps into which invaders were fatally beguiled, the mother of rich crops and malaria?

For us it presented an outstanding problem: how could we cross the depression? The friendly pylons swung even further away to where, in the distance, we could just see vehicles racing along the great northern highway.

Predictably unmarked on our maps were narrow roads and polders above the feeding-grounds of plovers, waders on stilts, sandpipers, oyster-catchers and dense flocks of small skittery marsh-hunters such as sanderlings that rose like smoke, uniformly turning and twisting in mid-air as if under a master command. High-speed photography attests there are many matters which, fortunately, we know next to nothing about. Man appeared, the first of its species we had seen that morning. He literally popped up on a very ancient motor-cycle propelled by one asthmatic cylinder. A friendly but rather fearsome-looking fellow with grey, black and gold teeth and a huge sack of beans strapped to his back. He switched off and all but fell off as he grasped my hands. To him, no doubt, we were also a rare if not entirely new species in that deserted country.

Good-days were exchanged before the ritual: where from? Where to? To the recommended *kafeneion* at Skourta, we said – had we the right road? His assurance was expressed as if by an exaggerated signing of the Cross, with the down-stroke giving us a visible bearing and the right to left, fortified by an agonized mime, indicating those paths which were to be *wholly* ignored. We were also promised a good and easy journey. He pointed to some birds, probably storks, flying high over a line of dead trees. From a chance meeting with an art-dealer in Thebes a day or two later I learnt that this classical form of divination still heralds good fortune to some country people.

Drinking mugs of tea brewed in the shade of a plane tree I thumbed through Pausanias' *Guide to Greece*. This doctor from Greek Asia Minor devoted nearly fifteen years to travelling in mainland Greece during and after the reign of Hadrian in the second century AD, 'the brief Golden Age of the Roman Empire'. Almost all that I know about this marvellously obsessed commentator comes from the translation and scholarly introduction by Peter Levi to the two-volume edition which, in his search for copious footnotes and what conditions are like today, suggest that he travelled as far as Pausanias did. As for the man who 'believed a ruined building was hardly worth mentioning', Mr Levi tell us that Pausanias belonged in Athens to a circle of almost professional antiquaries; he worked in great libraries; he consulted the sacred officials and city guides whom Plutarch describes at Delphi and who existed in every city. He appears to have been almost incessantly asking questions and writing, beginning when he had already passed middle age. In late life he became addicted to bird-watching and complained about steep hills and bad roads. Mr Levi suggests that his scholarship – he wrote in Greek for Roman philhellenes – and encyclopaedic curiosity were a burden undertaken in an attempt to satisfy a deeper anxiety which had been apprehended in religious terms. 'The collapse of ancient religion or some deeper collapse was the unspoken object of his studies. If this anxiety had not ridden him as it did, or had he been a less patient and learned traveller, modern archaeology would be immeasurably poorer' – and we should not have had such an informative travelling companion.

Pausanias says that the old kingdom of Boeotia, now a *nomos* or prefecture, was named after Boeotus, legendary son of Itonos by the nymph Melannipe who, according to another source, when she found herself with child by Aeolus, fled to Mount Pelion and was there metamorphosed by Artemis into a mare. The indefatigable doctor describes the rise and fall of Plataea to the south and between them the meandering of river Asopus which at one period divided the two kingdoms. He mentions sacred springs and divine objects called *daidala* made from oak wood. Five hundred years after the event, he writes of the crushing of the Spartan invaders at Leuctra by Boeotians under the mighty Epaminondas, and the decline of that war-ingrained race who, I suspect – on no good authority – took their name from the Spanish broom, *Sparteum junceum* which seems to have been as common in the Peloponnese as *Planta genista* in Anjou. Perhaps unknown to themselves, might not present-day Athenians still be celebrating the defeat of their traditional enemies by adorning their vehicles with bunches of broom on 1 May? Pausanias also writes of the building of the Seven Gates of Thebes to the sound of singing and the sweet noise of lyre and flutes. At the word 'singing' I heard, as if from long ago, a poignant aria which I have known since my father played the disc on his hand-cranked gramophone.

In his tuneful – if highly imaginative – version of *Orpheus in the Underworld*, Offenbach introduces King John who, among the shades below, catches a glimpse of Eurydice and immediately falls in love with her. But what can he offer a girl who is as dead as he is?

> *When I was King of Boeotia*
> *All my men were men of war.*
> *But then, alas, one day I died*
> *And all I owned were lost besides.*
> *Yet I can't pretend I really miss them.*
> *What in this place I really regret*

Is that I didn't choose you for bride.
But then, as I've said, alas I died.
If I were still King of Boeotia,
Upon my word you would be Queen.
But now you're offered in image only
All my royal power, yet
The finest shade, my darling,
Can offer you no more . . .

Poignant, but as I sang it under that Boeotian plane tree and apostrophized Katie in those last two lingering lines, a critical soul might have thought she seemed over-anxious to be off and away lest I sang it again.

The day wore on, slowly. No especial trauma at the village of Skourta if you are prepared to accept being rooked the equivalent of £5 for a plate of vegetables and a huge mound of what I suspect was goat liver. Why should we complain? We had asked neither the price nor the weight of the meat the fellow recommended. Fortunately we ate what we could in the open air where our presence attracted first one and then a horde of vicious cats who squabbled over the rubbery gobbets we were most anxious to be rid of.

To allow both the sun and our rumbling stomachs to lose their fervour we took a siesta in the shade of a jumble of rocks, and then were off again towards a distant horizon which could well have overlooked the sea. There is something that can almost always be said for the Greek scene and that is the abruptness with which it changes. Events were to prove that no matter whether we traced the rims of mountains or silently cursed the heat of a plain, we were constantly surprised by what could not be visually anticipated.

As we approached the cliff edge of our imagination the

horizon dissolved into a series of indefinable ridges until immediately below us stood a well-built farmhouse with outbuildings, beehives on a raised platform and an almost new tractor and a truck in a shed. We circled the house with its open doors. With dogs in mind we called out, loudly, but nobody answered, no dogs appeared. Handsome-looking horses grazed in an open field with a scampering of foals around the mares. Could this be the hamlet of Daphnoula, the only place marked on the map?

Mr Levi tells us that: 'almost all maps except old hoarded military staff sheets get you into more trouble than they get you out of.' However the road clearly ended at Daphnoula; it appeared to lead somewhere along our line of march and we followed its generous curves. We began to lose height, gradually. In a depression marked by an arc of reeds and sinuous willows, some diligent fellow, perhaps the owner of the horses with winter fodder in mind, had planted an extensive field of lucerne which had been invaded by poppies, vetches and other plants I couldn't recognize.

The field shimmered in the fierce light. The colour came from the soft gradations of violet and blue punctuated by the blood-red poppies, but the wonderful movement arose from undulations of hosts of butterflies, mostly members of the Blue family wholly at home on leguminous plants. Accustomed as we are to the scarcity of these beautiful creatures on the poisoned soils of post-war Britain, we were favoured, it seemed, by a glimpse of a prelapsarian state of affairs. In their urge to copulate, innumerable spires of the Least blue (*Cupido minimus*) arose and fell like will-o'-the-wisps; the Osiris blue (*C. osiris*) seemed more intent on laying eggs on the trefoil leaves of the lucerne than sipping nectar from the short spikes of its flowers.

By far the commonest species was that butterfly so rarely seen nowadays on the English Downs, the fast-flying Long-tailed blue (*Lampides boeticus*) which can be identified only between its urgent migrations. Large and Small coppers (*Lycaena*), Clouded yellows (*Colias*) and large numbers of Cabbage whites (*Pieris*) hovered over the huge thistles, daisies and miniature chrysanthemums around the lucerne. On the bark of a pink-flowered Judas tree I caught a glimpse of that spectacular butterfly with lace-edged wings, the Camberwell Beauty (*Nymphalis antiope*) once known as the Great Surprise because of its unexpected and striking appearance.

That afternoon I seemed touched by the wand of youth as I recalled days absorbed by the pursuit of insects in our northern dales. By unravelling the scientific names of creatures brought home alive in match-boxes and the celluloid tubes of the manufacturers of Beecham's pills I picked up a nodding acquaintanceship with the classics, since the names of most insects were taken from Greek or Latin mythology. Carl von Linné (1707–78) introduced the foreshortened, the scientific binomial. When his predecessor, John Ray (1627–1705), wished to allude to the Peacock butterfly he had been obliged to describe it as '*Papilio elegantissima ad Urticarium accedens, singulis alis singulis maculis oculos imitantibus perbelle depictis*'. 'A most handsome butterfly that frequents stinging nettles with a spot painted most beautifully on each wing so as to resemble an eye'. Thereafter, in order to make his meaning quite clear, he went on to mention the name or descriptions given by Petiver, Mouffet and Goedart, and also the English name. For the man who Latinized his name to Linnaeus, a bare two words sufficed, *Nymphalis io*, which, however irrelevantly, commemorates the daughter of an otherwise forgotten King of Argos.

Similarly, the scientific name of the Least blue (*Cupido minimus*) is derived from Cupid or Eros, the trouble-making son of Aphrodite; the Long-tailed blue carries the suggestion of its flame-like quality, *Lampides* meaning a torch or flambeau. I can't imagine what the Coppers, both large and small (*Lycaena*), have to do with the she-wolf: the word is probably Lucaios, a town in Arcadia; whilst many of the Whites (*Pieris*) are named after the Muses who were reputedly born in Pieria under Mount Olympos. Pedantic perhaps, but *Pieris* sounds better than Cabbage White.

After another three hours of walking our meandering road led us to the village of Pili where, more tired than we should have been, we sought comfort in a noisy though hospitable tavern. More than anything else we had a mind to sit quietly over a bottle of wine. It didn't work out that way. No sooner had the good woman of the house put down the retsina and the usual titbits, biscuits, olives and the like, than a precocious little moppet put her head round the door. Seeing we were alone she shouted and skipped in with her friends. We made polite gestures of disapproval. Imagining them to be some form of greeting they imitated my upraised hands and ferocious grin. The first moppet said, 'Me English spik. Me from Thivai [Thebes] come.' Not wishing to be outclassed the rest of the children danced round our table chanting first the English alphabet and then fragments of our multiplication tables.

In the midst of the hullabaloo an old man walked in, dismissed the children with a few sharp words which it would have been wise to have memorized, sat down and began to interrogate us in a wheezy voice. He was joined by a priest and the village blacksmith, Nicos, who had spent ten years on Clydeside. It came out that the oldster, a professional soldier, had fought the Germans under the name of the National Liberation Front, EAM. 'Where?' I asked. 'First here,' said Nicos, translating, 'and then on Mount Parnis. I was only quite young when the bastards came in with an infantry patrol, two armoured cars and a light tank.'

Had I been a soldier? I nodded. He spoke rapidly to the old man. They beckoned me outside where, by pointing out landmarks with his stick, the old soldier – over eighty – described how with advance warning they had mined the road in several places, overturned the armour and killed or wounded most of the infantry before he and his neighbours took to the hills. Reprisals followed. Among several adolescents who had never handled a rifle, three of his relatives were lined up against a wall and shot. 'We were lucky,' Nicos said. 'Father took us up to the Kliston *monastiri* above Phyle.'

Before we returned to our table I asked Nicos whether the priest had joined the *Andartes*, the Resistance fighters. He hesitated before replying. 'No,' he said with echoes of Maryhill and Sauchiehall Street in his voice. 'He wasn't a *papas* until the Germans were kicked out. He was a young novice in the monastery during the invasion. After that . . .' He shrugged his shoulders.

With a murmured blessing and hopes for a good journey the priest left us. The old man followed him. Katie walked through to the kitchen for a word with our hostess about food, leaving me to talk to Nicos alone. I wanted to unravel the ground plan of that terrible affair, the civil war when brothers in divided villages fought against each other, and wondered how to begin. As if reading my thoughts he asked about the strength of the Communist Party in Britain. Weak in numbers, I said, but the big unions had small if influential groups of what we called the Hard Left, and I added, 'unfortunately'. He half rose and banged the table with his fist. 'It's the same everywhere,' he said, his voice rising. 'We are still contaminated.'

Within minutes I learnt that he supported Papandreou and PASOK, the Pan Hellenic Socialist Movement. He would have preferred Mitsotakis, the leader of New Democracy: 'A tough Cretan who doesn't try to please everybody,' he said. Before Katie returned with our supper wrapped up in a Theban newspaper, he gave me local examples of how the Resistance movement, EAM, developed on Russian lines with Russian arms and became an organized army (ELAS) and even a navy (ELAN). The Communists formed their own trade union organization (EEAM), a Youth Movement (EPON), a Cooperative Society (EA), a Secret Police (OPLA) and a Civil Guard (EP). In Greece there are not a few passionate politicians. They are all passionate politicians.

I returned to the subject of priests actually carrying arms. Nicos grinned. In his opinion there were more rifles in monasteries than anywhere else. On the island of Chios the most successful guerrilla force was raised, organized and led by a priest. According to Osbert Lancaster, many years ago, in the notoriously violent Mani country, the participation of priests in blood feuds was governed by certain well-defined laws. As he put it: 'Thus while Holy Orders were not in themselves regarded as sufficient to remove a priest from the category of fair game, the Man of God could not be potted while actually officiating behind the iconostasis. On the other hand he was obliged to remove whatever firearms he carried beneath his cope before approaching the altar.'

Nicos asked us where we intended to spend the night. My turn to shrug. Why not above his foundry, he asked. We could then have breakfast together and meet the man who led the local Resistance. I was obliged to go through the ritual excuses about getting away early but he did give us valuable advice about a track to head for the next day. With out supper in the newspaper and another bottle of wine the colour of honey, price about twenty-five pence, we walked out into the murky dusk. What turns everything to majesty in Greece is the sunlight; when that goes everything seems to shrivel in the dark.

We might have slept under the stars if we had realized how warm it was. The inner fly started to perspire. Cold drops of water fell on us until we took the sheet down in the dark. Then came a mysterious scratching noise. Something appeared to be moving under my portion of the sleeping-bag. A mole cricket, I thought, or maybe a field mouse. Katie woke up as I tried to locate the creature. Nothing visible by torch light. We slept, fitfully, until she woke me again saying that something seemed to be moving under the waterproofs and a cloth that served as her pillow. Whenever we moved the scratching noise ceased and we tried to ignore it.

From that morning onwards we usually packed our gear after a frugal sponging down, postponing coffee and something to eat until we had limbered up and got into the swing of things. The sight of a river meandering under the early-morning sun looked tempting and to the sound of more frogs than I have ever heard before we stopped for breakfast.

I lifted Katie's pack off her shoulders, winced at the weight of it, and inched off my own. Too heavy by far. Mentally running over what could be left behind at Thebes I turned at her half-suppressed cry. As she pulled out the cloth wrapped round the butane stove, a red centipede, the biggest I have seen, a flat creature about eight inches in length, fell to the ground and scuttled off. At the time, that is between lighting the cooker and enjoying the fried bacon, bread and coffee, I thought it best not to say too much about the thing, not least because I know the species can bite if provoked. Centipedes have never been among my familiars but frogs now, there's as merry a crew as ever brightened me up when affairs haven't been at their best. A professional observer, Dr Archie Carr, once wrote: 'I like the faces of frogs. I like their outlook and especially the way they get together in warm wet places and sing about sex.'

Among the reedy shallows of the meandering Asopus, a classical stream much written about by Pausanias as the boundary between inter-Boeotian rivals, Thebes and Plataea, a legion of multi-coloured frogs were at an amphibian version of the 'Hallelujah Chorus'. They leaped from beneath our footsteps on a marshy bank strewn with purple iris and saffron-eyed daisies; they splashed down among their fellows with their forelegs interlocked under the bellies of fertilized females: gloriously green frogs, goggle-eyed and seemingly grinning frogs, acrobatic frogs with two sometimes three mates struggling to get down to copulation. *Kama Sutra?* Not for nothing have these intergraded hybrids been given the scientific name of *Rana epierotica*.

The chorus defies easy description. Enough to say that through the cheeps, peeps and tremolos came the belchy bass notes which haven't changed since Aristophanes described the noise over 2,000 years ago in his bawdy and vastly entertaining comedy, *The Frogs: Brekeke-kex-ko-ax, ko-ax*. Behind the vulgarities his theme is a serious one. As a recent translator, David Barrett describes the scene: 'In January 405 BC Athens was not a cheerful city. At Dekelea, only a few miles away, the Spartans lay encamped. Not many months before, they had marched right up to the city walls, 30,000 strong, and the Athenians had only just managed to man the defences in time. And now Lysander, the Spartan admiral, supported by Cyrus the Persian, was preparing for the spring offensive in which he hoped to inflict the final blow on the Athenian fleet.'

Behind the mask of the comedian, Aristophanes creates a completely farcical situation which begins on the outskirts of Athens and ends in Hades, suggesting that during that crucial period the two realms weren't all that far apart. One by one the characters, both the living and the dead, the mythical and the real, including Euripides, Charon,

Aeschylus, Pluto and Dionysus, the patron god of drama,
engage in mock-serious debate derided by the chorus of
frogs: *Brekeke-kex-ko-ax, ko-ax* – which might be put across
today as *Blah Blah Blah*! Dionysus tells them to shut up.

> *Now listen, you musical twerps,*
> *I don't give a damn for your burps!*

He is exhausted. He has rowed across the lake.

> *What a sweat! I'm all wet! What a bore!*
> *I'm so raw! I'm so sore! And what's more,*
> *Some blisters have come on my delicate bum*
> *Where I've never had blisters before.* *

With enormous skill Aristophanes blends uncommon sense
with outrageous slapstick. What he is really getting at, says
Mr Barrett, is that the City is in great danger. Unless the
Athenians can find advisers who are both wise and moral
and not merely clever fellows they will perish, swallowed
by a system which hasn't worked. With little profit to the
State they have listened to politicians and orators: isn't it
about time they listened to other advisers? What about the
poets? In that much quoted line Aristophanes says: 'School-
boys have a master to teach them, grown-ups have the
poets.'

With the pocket-recorder and field glasses at the ready
we clung to the Asopus for mile after mile to get the best
of the sounds and riotous scenes in the river below. Various
warblers and orioles contributed to the chorus but they were
as nought by comparison with that massive frolic of frog-
dom. It led us astray. By following a wayward tributary we

* *Aristophanes, The Wasps, The Poet and The Women, The Frogs*, David
Barrett, Penguin Books, 1964.

all but missed the city of Thebes and were obliged to retrace our steps by some three or four miles, much of it through calf-deep mud on a flood plain.

Down an inconspicuous side lane we squelched up to the predictably unmapped hamlet of Neohoraki devoted almost entirely, as far as we could make out, to the growth, extraction and transport of wayside alps of pink potatoes in the process of being shovelled up by some very friendly natives. Shouts of welcome. Handshakes all round. The innkeeper's apologies for not being able to offer us more than a dollop of the for-ever-simmering cauldron of mutton stew were interrupted by the arrival of a van-load of sardines, loudly proclaimed by bursts of recorded bouzouki music audible, we reckoned, at a radius of half a mile. Mildly deafened but satisfied by grilled fish, fried potatoes and immoderate flasks of retsina, we rested awhile before soldiering on through landscapes of Boeotian spuds.

The tracks were far from straightforward since the Neohorakians made it clear that anybody in their right mind would head for the main road just visible on the horizon. Some fibrous roots tripped me up, twice. An overladen man stumbles easily. Katie's ankles were deeply scratched by heavily armoured thistles. In short, we were up against Ventre's stark dictum that *les choses sont contre nous*. Resistentialism. No matter. We struck a tolerably surfaced side road and quickened pace when a signpost half promised that we were within two kilometres of sacred Thebes of the Seven Gates, birthplace of Dionysus, Hercules and all that lot.

The dramatic moments of life are apt to fall singularly flat. Neither of us had been to Thebes before. On several occasions I had been driven to Delphi but it had always been by chartered buses or the equivalent of American

69

Greyhounds which bypass the town by two miles on their way to Livadia and the roller-coaster road to Delphi. Had I spent more time on Pausanias and less on the flora and geology of Greece we should not have been so disappointed by the rather shabby quarter of a rather shabby town. For years I had been carried away by the prospect of the Seven Gates first mentioned by Homer in the eleventh book of the *Odyssey*, the Book of the Dead. The world's first story-teller and, surely, one of the greatest in the world, relates how Athena, Goddess of the Flashing Eyes and Circe, Mistress of the Magic Arts gave Odysseus of the Nimble Wits precise instructions about how to reach the Shades below where, he was told, he could assuage 'the enmity of Poseidon, the Earth-shaker, brother of Zeus who had for so long kept Odysseus in exile, unable to return home to Ithaca and the faithful bed of his bride, Penelope, beseiged in her own home by a horde of amorous and ambitious princelings.

The Earth-shaker has always seemed to me to be a petty, broody fellow and it doesn't require Freud to explain what Homer knew by instinct – that Poseidon should suffer from nephew resentment, not least because the Gatherer of Clouds had described the gallant young wanderer as 'not only the bravest man alive but the one most generous to the immortals who live in heaven'. I used the first three words of a poem by Andrew Lang for the title of the first book I ever wrote*, the reminiscences of a youthful fisherman.

> *Within the Streams, Pausanias sayeth,*
> *That down the Cocytus valley flow,*
> *Girdling the grey domain of death,*
> *The spectral fishes come and go;*

---

* *Within the Streams*, Harvey and Blyth, London, 1949.

> *The ghosts of trout flit to and fro.*
> *Persephone, fulfil my wish,*
> *And grant that in the shades below*
> *My ghost may catch the ghosts of fish.*

Horace, in his old age and on a well-deserved pension from Maecenas, wrote: 'Often on a work of grave purpose and high promise is tacked a purple patch or two to give an effect of colour.'

The story is that Odysseus brought his blue-prowed ship into the deep-flowing River of Ocean, the frontier of the world where the fog-bound Cimmerians live in the City of Perpetual Mist and dreadful Night has spread her mantle over the heads of that unhappy crew. There the wanderer, exiled son of Laertes, encountered first his old companion Elpenor and then the spirit of blind Tiresias, most famous of the Theban prophets who told him how he might overcome fearful obstacles on his way back to Ithaca and what he should do when he arrived there. Odysseus thanked him. He admitted that the threads of destiny could not be cut since the gods themselves had spun them. Yet he begged to be allowed to speak to the spirit of his dead mother, Anticlea, wife of Laertes, who had been in good health when he sailed for Troy, and also to other high-born souls with the ability to tell him something about the strange relationship between the gods and men and the cities they built – such as Thebes when she ruled the greater part of Greece.

His royal mother wept at the sight of her grievously travel-worn son, not least because being a spirit without sinews and bones to hold her flesh together she could not embrace him. Yet she told him how she had died out of heart-ache for her shining first-born and she comforted him with news of his resolute wife, Penelope and their son, Telemachus, ever-watchful and constantly at her call.

We said very little as we climbed up a steep hill towards

what should have been the Hypsistai Gate on the Southern approach to the Kadmeia at the centre of the city reputedly founded by Cadmus the Phoenician. Not a gate, not a tower in sight. We were in a nondescript quarter devoted mostly to the sale of meat, vegetables and bathroom appliances. With fantasies mildly encouraged we struck along Pindarou Street – once the home, possibly, of Pindar, one of the greatest lyric poets of Greece whose house was spared when Alexander sacked the city. Enthusiasms were stirred slightly when we crossed Dirkis Street for this, surely, was associated with that unfortunate woman Dirce who, for some reason I have forgotten, was killed by Amphion and Zethus who tied her to the horns of a bull understandably enraged by having its balls interfered with.

On what we hoped were more certain grounds we passed Oedipus Street on our left and another to the right named after his daughter, Antigone (O shades of Sophocles), who led her incestuous and self-blinded father to Colonus where she buried him before taking her own life. Can one be surprised that to the name of no other city of antiquity does there cling so romantic and so ominous an aura as that praised by Homer for its gates? But where were they?

I put the question to a swarthy young policeman: *Parakalo. Pou ine oi epta portes?* He looked surprised. Did we want a good restaurant with many doors? No, I said, no! *Ohi!* Clearly he didn't know what I was talking about. With the same result we tried the man with a tall wooden crucifix which fluttered with dozens of raffle tickets, a fishmonger and a waiter in a small bar who motioned us to an outside table and returned with an old man to interpret.

At my elaborate explanation about the great city of Thebes of a long time ago, he smiled hugely. The drachma had dropped. He pointed down Pindarou Street and said, 'The museum!' But, alas, it was being made new again and would not be open for many months. We sighed. He sighed but brightened up at my suggestion that a drink might be good for all of us. As we ate a small meal there and refreshed his glass I asked about a good hotel, not too far away. At this he closed one eye and with his forefinger pointed straight up into the darkening sky. I looked at Katie and she, practical as ever, stepped into the middle of the road and looked around. 'He's quite right,' she said. 'The Hotel Meletiouy is almost upstairs.'

Within minutes we had dumped our packs, handed in our passports, braved the creaking lift, pulled off our sweaty clothes, taken a shower and sunk into what seemed centuries of sleep on a super-pneumatic bed of eider feathers.

We awoke to find the world new-made and shining. A shabby town did I say? From the street level, as we had discovered the previous evening, there are few architectural prizes to be won in modern Thebes because the best-known town in Boeotia stands on a huge mound, a natural fortress. Rusty iron stairs from our balcony led up to a flat roof where, far beyond a richly covered riot of pantiled roofs, we saw a ring of distant mountains, pale purple in the early morning light: Kithairon to the south, Helicon due west, Thourion and Chlomon to the north and Ptoon and Messapion to the north-east, relieved by sparkles of light from the Euboean Gulf.

We were far from alone. High above, like a cloud of gnats, countless hundreds of swifts screamed around us, some of them so close that we could hear the whirr of their sickle-shaped wings. We clambered down to our room, gingerly, since our underfootings were sore and lightly blistered which, to a professional walker, is as adultery in a priest. Leaving Katie with a light breakfast and three days' laundry to attend to, I suggested we should meet again in an hour or two and took a town stroll, alone but not for long.

The swarthy cop, talking to Stefano, our helpful

informant, gripped my arms as if on a serious charge. Through rapid interpretation he enquired whether we found our lodgings favourable. 'Very good,' I said. This clearly pleased Stefano since it turned out that the wife of the patron, apparently a rich woman, was their favourite aunt on his mother's side. Greek scales of familiarity tend to be biased in favour of the prospect of a rich inheritance.

Parting from my two companions with some difficulty I walked up Epameinondou Street, north, towards the museum, fascinated by the number of shops devoted to flamboyant if not downright vulgar bathroom appliances. Baths, bidets and basins in pink marble were commonplace, eclipsed only by a big store which gave a whole window to a huge lemon-coloured jacuzzi that, the manufacturers claimed, could be filled in fifteen seconds by pressing a gilded console.

Most of the general stores in Thebes add to the fun in the Boeotian bathroom by offering a great variety of soaps, bath salts, fragrant oils and unguents presumably supporting John Wesley's curious belief in the relationship between cleanliness and godliness.

Just off Kevitas Street is a *plateia* nicely framed by ancient planes and mulberry trees where, hearing the ringing, the almost trumpet-like call of a Golden oriole, I forgot about the museum and sat down to coffee and brittle rolls together with a shot of superior Greek brandy (Votrys) the better to digest them. Tiring of the three-day-old edition of the *International Herald Tribune* I took out the micro-recorder and whispered into it *sotto voce* much to the admiration of the waiter who thought, I suppose, that I was speaking to Athens or London by radio telephone. Why, I asked that useful little machine, were the Thebans so addicted to soap? Could it be that hygiene is the corruption of the conscience by notions about external cleanliness? Pliny the Elder wrote that the Phoenicians were the first to prepare the stuff that makes you a little lovelier each day from goats' tallow and wood ashes. Now wasn't Cadmus, who is said to have founded Thebes, a Phoenician, who might well have brought soap in addition to the first use of letters in Greece to that very Kadmeia in which I sat? Didn't he sow the dragon's teeth? By persuading commoners to soap off what their best friends wouldn't tell them, he was perhaps among the first to wash civilizations down the drain. I began to warm to the proposition. Votrys is evocative stuff.

I thought of Rome where the inhabitants became so obsessed with lying around in hot baths that they could no longer face sleeping out on cold battle-fields and thus fell prey to unwashed barbarians. I thought of modern America under the spell of J. Walter Thompson and Procter and Gamble. Mark Twain said something to the effect that soap and education are not as sudden as massacres but they are more deadly in the long run. I wondered if during our finest hours we in Britain could have tolerated Goering's fire-raisers but for the fact that soap was rationed and we were limited to five inches of bath water.

Two splendid birds like enormous butterflies floated down from the crown of one of the plane trees. They were pinkish-brown hoopoes crested in the manner of a Mycenaean lord in battle-dress. They alighted on a patch of rough ground which they began to probe with their long curved bills. When they found something succulent, a caterpillar or a beetle perhaps, they crooned with evident delight: '*pou-pou-pou*' which is good Greek – as even I know since I had been saying it so often – for 'where? where? where?' That deeply melodic call can be imitated almost precisely by blowing a gentle staccato across the mouth of an empty wine bottle.

The birds, probably a mated pair whose fledgelings had gone off on their own, were not only superior-looking, as if conscious of their fine plumes and matching gowns, sable and argent from the shoulders down, but also seemed downright *fond* of each other. They fed close together and when they weren't amicably *pou-pouing*, the male or maybe the female (since the sexes are virtually indistinguishable) would give a hiccupy *gloop* suggesting possibly that a beetle had gone down the wrong way.

Inevitably *Eupupa epops*, to give the creatures their endearing scientific name, have figured heavily if wholly improbably in Greek mythology. Tereus, son of Ares, the god of war and not to be confused with Tiresias, the bisexual soothsayer of Thebes, brought up his commandos in support of Pandion, King of Attica who had got himself into difficulties in a local shenanigan. With help from the Immortals Pandion won hands down, and in gratitude married off to Tereus his rich daughter, Procne and she bore him a son, Itys. Unfortunately for all concerned, Tereus fell in love with the voice of his sister-in-law, Philomela who resisted him. So he raped her on the side. Affairs thereafter got more than somewhat gruesome, even by classical standards.

Procne, his wife, got wind of the affair and to stop her blabbing Tereus cut out her tongue. Planning revenge on her barbarous husband, she slew their child Itys and served him up to Tereus for supper. When he rumbled what had happened, he picked up his axe and chased the sisters to Daulis on the road to Thebes. There he might have killed them both, but the gods intervened. They turned Philomela into the nightingale who forever mourns the death of Itys in her throbbing song: '*Tereu, Tereu, Itu, Itu*'; Procne into the swallow that twitters and flies round in circles but cannot speak; whilst Tereus became the hoopoe flying in pursuit of them, crying *Pou, pou, pou* – where? where?

To my mild annoyance the birds flew off at the approach of a misty-blue Mercedes, a quietly luxurious car bearing Swiss plates. It turned round in near its own length, reversed and purred to a standstill in a shadow which might have been made for it. The driver, a trim-bearded fellow in his sixties, as handsome as his car, stepped out, apparently with some difficulty. He limped over. He glanced at my copy of the *Herald Trib*, lowered his head, politely, and said, 'Good morning, *M'sieur.*'

Since I yearned for someone to talk to and because, too, he fitted my notion of Svengali, I suggested he might care to join me over a coffee. Within an hour I had learnt much about Thebes and a little about the intriguing activities of an exotic art-dealer.

Born in Famagusta of Turko-Jewish parents and now a naturalized citizen of Ascona, M. Théophane, to disclose only the received portion of his name, could fairly be described as an extremely knowledgeable exquisite. Wisely worldly, not the other way round. His car, dress, idiom and other lightly worn jewellery were all of a piece.

'What brings you to Thebes?' he asked.

Dressed as I was in tourist gadabouts, a respectable pullover, jeans and open sandals, I told him, briefly – we were going to Southern Macedonia on foot. We had a mind to see at least the summit of Mount Olympos. He looked down at my sandals. '*Mais c'est une grande tournée,*' he said. 'There is between here and your destination some considerable difficulties. Have you experience in these matters?' I told him I had been to many countries, always on foot.

He paused before saying: '*On dit que* the man who takes long steps is obliged to turn his back on large spaces.'

'Is that Islamic?'

He shook his head. 'From Malaysia. I was in Borneo, among the Dyaks.'

What had he been looking for? He smiled before saying, 'Whatever is of value. The fetish figures, amulets of jadeite and human heads, but shrunken of course.'

'Rather gruesome, eh?'

77

'*Peit-être, mais j'ai payé cher.*'

'How much?'

He sighed before he slapped his thigh. 'With this. The polyneuritis. I was on crutches and it was three years before I could walk without a stick.' I tried to turn the conversation back to Thebes, but mentally Théophane was still in the tropics. 'In the Belgian Congo it was acute dysentery and in Peru yellow fever,' he said. 'Have you visited there?'

'To the Congo for several months – up and down the river twice in the Belgian days. But never to South America. What did you find there?'

'*Beaucoup de choses*, including this,' he said, stretching out his second finger, encircled as it was by a small but exquisite ring of bright green malachite set in silver. There were deep incisions on the square face of the stone which I couldn't make out.

'That is from Cuzco, an Inca seal ring cut in the great days of Huayua Capac, *c'est à dire* before Pizarro arrived early in the sixteenth *siècle* when he began to destroy the first and probably the most successful socialistic government in the world. It lasted for three *siècles*, almost. Had I another ring like this I could buy a super-Ferrari, that is, if I wanted one. *Mais non*, I prefer the ring. It has a rather curious history. Look at the engraving, like a labyrinth, no? The squares represent numbers. The Incas had some acquaintance of Pythagoras. That is of no surprise to me. So did the architects of your megalithic monuments in 2,000 BC. You can draw an immense stone circle with the equivalent of string but not a precise oval, where you are obliged to understand the properties of right-angled triangles. Only one other ring resembles this one, that I know, and that is in the museum at Ankara. One dug it up in Anatolia.'

'At Çatal Hüyük?'

He laughed outright. '*Mon Dieu, non!* So you know the story of what is perhaps the oldest roofed city in the world,

6,000 BC eh? And the missing jewellery which – how shall I put it? Shall we say, implicated one of your fellow countrymen?' He laughed again. 'Yes, I have been to Çatal Hüyük and nearby Hacilar in the Taurus mountains. I have good stuff from there. But I am an honest dealer, *vous savez*, not an archaeologist.'

'But what's the connection between the two rings?' I asked. 'Arab traders,' he said. 'They took their dhows across the Atlantic not long after, possibly even before the Vikings. For the purposes of barter is it not likely that they presented the Incas with mystical drawings including algebra from Byzantium? Pythagoras died in 500 BC *tout à fait* obsessed with ideas about the immortality of the soul and its transmigrations. That would appeal to the Incas. Much came from Anatolia and Phoenicia.'

He stroked the ring with affection. 'In the period between the second millennium and the second century before Christ, Greece gave to Europe its first poets, its first dramatists, its first architects, first historians, first philosophers and first scientists. It developed ideas on reasoning, democracy, and even the first notion of a universe composed of atoms in perpetual motion. The cultures came, *à l'origine*, from sources as far apart as Mongolia, Upper Egypt, Minoan Crete, Anatolia and Phoenicia.'

'By what routes?' I asked.

He lifted his arms in an eloquent Turko-Gallic gesture. '*Je ne sais pas*,' he said, 'at least not with precision. But then nobody else does. If I did know I would not fly around the world like a mad magpie picking up expensive trinkets. It is for me not possible perhaps to walk for more than a few hundred metres, but movement of any kind is a substitute for making the decisions, as premiers and presidents know. It assists me to keep intellectually alive.'

'What on earth did the Mongolians contribute?' I asked.

'*Beaucoup*,' he said. 'You have heard, *sans doute*, of the

Scythians – or the Kindred-Scyths as the anthropologists call
them to confuse the record in case they are challenged?
They were a race or confederation of warrior-horsemen,
perhaps the first to domesticate that striped wild beast named
after Prewaltski. They dominated a vast crescent of the
steppe which stretched from the Wall of China to the banks
of the Danube. They were known to, they were feared by
the great Darius, the father of Xerxes, who started the long
war between Persia and Attica. He had seen samples of
smelted gold in bars from a royal treasury in the Altai
mountains. A Russian called Radlov found some of it about
a hundred years ago. Since then there have been located
and excavated several frozen tombs known as *kurgans*; one
of them at Pazryk disclosed the tattooed body of an elderly
warrior, probably a prince who had died of battle wounds.
Alongside him lay a woman, *bien-tonne* but frigid of course,
his consort slain by ceremony. Objects of *grande* value
included gold-inlaid war apparatus, armour and the like,
sacrificial tablets, musical instruments, portable furniture
made of Chinese sandalwood, carpets, jewellery, cosmetics
and hashish burners. Today, the material, including the
bodies of the royal Scyths, is all in the Hermitage museum
in Leningrad. I have seen it. I should like to visit the Altai
mountains – but do you suppose the Russians would admit
a trader who is *assez bien connu*?

'The Scyths attained the Balkans where they clashed with
and were beaten by the Thracians who absorbed much of
their culture, in particular in what today is Bulgaria.
Heredotus tells us that the Thracians were a people made
for war who, if they had been united under a single king,
would have been invincible. He says also that each man
who could afford the luxury had several wives and practised
barbarous customs. When the warrior-husbands died, the
women made dispute among themselves with some violence
to decide which one he loved most so that she could be

buried with him. The Thracians used to hold regular lotteries and the winner – if that is what one may call him – was thrown up in the air by his comrades so that he landed on upturned javelins. He was given instructions to let their great god Zalmoxis know what is was on earth that they most desired that year. If the *pauvre homme* died, they thought the god would grant their wishes. But if he did not die, at least within the few hours that they stood around and watched him in silence, they blamed him, saying he was an unreliable man, and after the rising and the setting of the moon during a certain season they drew lots to decide who should be the next hero-victim.

'The Thracians reached Greece where they were counter-attacked by veritably *tout le monde* from the Macedonians to the Romans. They had no written language but some strange ceremonials and their history was depicted on golden cups and tablets. One of them* shows a huge double door, *un peu entr'ouvert* to reveal the head and forearms of a terrified old man. A small group of armed warriors almost as tall as the door are advancing upon him with upraised Thracian swords and expressions of murder.' He paused for a second for dramatic emphasis and slowly lifted his forefinger. '*Écoutez*, could not that be the story of the Seven Against Thebes?'

'Do you think the huge door could be one of the seven gates?' I asked.

'*Non*. I do not believe there were ever seven gates to this city.'

'But Homer talks about them in the Book of the Dead and Pausanias claims he saw them. We have brought Levi's translation with us.'

'I suggest you reread it with more care,' he said. 'Seven Gates has the sound of mythology. Seven is a mystical

---

* *Part of the Penagurishte treasure in Sofia.*

number: the Seven Heavens, the Seven Sacraments, the Seven Joys of Mary, the Seven Liberal Arts, the Gods of Luck, the Hills of Rome, Seven Seas, Seven Sleepers, the Seven Deadly Sins – I could make it twelve. Seven Gates would be very difficult to defend, but three would have offered access to their principal roads: north to Thessaly including the port of Vathi from which we believe the fleet sailed for Troy; south to Athens; and west to Delphi along the Sacred Way. How do you propose to get there, might I ask?'

'Tomorrow we shall head for the southern rim of Mount Helicon and then west to the port of Itea below Delphi,' I said.

He sighed. 'Even if my legs were in good condition I should prefer the comfort of my car. I think there is little of the noble and virtuous in the cultivation of blisters. No matter. Nietzsche is of your opinion. His thought was that a sedentary life is the real sin against the Holy Spirit. He says our finest thoughts come to us when we push one foot in front of the other, slowly, as we are thinking.'

He rose to go and held out his hand. '*M'sieur*, it has been a privilege to talk to you. But I have business here. The key to much that has happened in the past still lies in this town, but do you suppose Thebans with their minds of commerce are prepared to let people burrow like moles for the chance of finding a few objects which are likely to be carried off to the museum in Athens? *Heureusement*, there are a few who have embraced archaeology for non-scholastic reasons and I am one of their patrons. My respects to Madame in her heroic exercise, and good luck to you both.' He limped towards his mist-blue car. He waved briefly from the side window and drove off.

Katie sat on the balcony surrounded by our almost dry laundry. Before I could tell her much about the dealer from Ascona she said: 'I have news for you. In one of his footnotes to Pausanias, your friend Mr Levi suggests that the Seven Gates were not the gates to classical Thebes but to the Kadmeia, the ancient acropolis, a sort of shrine within a city. And perhaps there were only three. The others might have been invented by Aeschylus. I have looked him up. It fits in nicely with his *Seven Against Thebes*.'

Fruits of the Earth

We were alone again but not for long. Half a mile beyond the city limits I found that I had carried off the huge brass key to our hotel bedroom and, worse, I'd forgotten to pick up our passports. Taking off that heavy sack and leaving Katie with a book in the sanctuary of a mosque-like church, I strode back, peevishly, to the hotel receptionist, a pretty chubby girl whose Danish name sounded something like Moll Flanders, a fanciful notion heightened by her truly hypertrophic bosom which had put one of us in mind of the famous snake goddess in topless garb I'd seen in pictures of Knossos. I walked there and back far too fast, and felt out of sorts when we set off again.

Our friends, including the helpful cop, had assured us that our little road, not unlike an open lane in Devon, would take us to the steep southern flanks of Mount Helicon which plunge into the Gulf of Corinth. The carefully tended fields devoted to foraging flocks, ancient olives, vines pruned to within two feet of the red soil, vegetables various and a pale green haze of newly emerging corn were refreshed by whirling sprays that clicked and hissed above the screech of young starlings. Not my favourite bird. Among the furrows they made me think of lice in the seams of a tramp's clothing.

Here and there, usually in the vicinity of whitewashed

farmsteads, could be seen the dark green foliage of mulberry trees on which, for many centuries, the Boeotians fed their silkworms. There is reasonable evidence that in the seventh century those industrious caterpillars were smuggled into the Byzantine empire from China by two monks who combined religious zealotry with a practical devotion to the principles of free trade. Until the Bulgarians sacked the city in 1040, Thebes could be regarded as the Lyons of the Eastern Mediterranean. After its resurrection by the lordly Burgundians and Franks, Theban silk became a staple probably more widely known, certainly no less valuable than Cistercian wool.

No silk is now produced there but, as I learnt from the knowledgeable M. Théophane, the fertile plain around the city is still known to oldsters as the Morocampus and the surviving trees, mostly *Morus alba*, could well be the descendants of the purple-encased seeds sown at the beginning of the Theban Renaissance under Nicholas de St Omer and his youthful liege lord, the extremely well-connected Duke of Athens. Thickly clothed mulberries make efficient windbreaks, the leaves are used for feeding livestock, but most trees are cherished, I suspect, because the fruit is the source of a bootleg liquor known as *moru*.

For some botanical reason beyond easy comprehension the raspberry-like mulberry is a fairly close relative of the fig. They are gastronomically neglected since they combine the extremes of squashiness and pippiness, though the flavour, searchingly sour and hauntingly sweet, comes out best in the liqueur. In a stylish restaurant it should be asked for by tapping your lower lip and saying with quiet authority: '*Thelo na soo mileeso moru, parakalo.*'

The morning wore on and when we began to gain height, almost imperceptibly, the soil looked stony and less fertile. The terraced vines appeared to be fighting for survival. Patches of corn and parched vegetables were protected from itinerant goats by formidable palisades of cactus, the prickly pear. From the numbers of highly poisonous plants thereabouts, such as *Hyoscyamus*, the white henbane; *Mandragora* or mandrake which was supposed to shriek when dug up, 'a noyse that spells death to incautious delvers'; and Datura or thorn apple, with its white trumpet-shaped flowers, I wondered if that particular soil was contaminated, possibly by arsenic.

A curious thing about many poisonous plants is that, even to those innocent of their lethal properties, they look downright unpleasant. Who, for example, would pluck and chew the black cherries of the Deadly Nightshade not uncommon in our chalk quarries in company with Old Man's Beard, the wild clematis? Yet my old friend the Alchemist* assured me that a fearful outbreak of poisoning causing several deaths occurred in London in the last century when the fruit was offered for sale under the novelty name of Nettleberries by an urban vendor who was either ignorant or without a conscience, or both, since the plant has been known as Dwale, Doleful Bells or the Devil's Cherries. He was subsequently convicted of manslaughter.

Few trees could be seen except the pink-flowered *Cercis* or Judas tree on which the Iscariot is said to have hanged himself. According to legend, the flowers still blush. The junipers clung to the ground and olives had reverted to their wild form. They were fruitful but when, once and for all time, I bit into one they were as bitter and tongue-tingling as something between aloes and sloes. I should have known better. They were festooned with small yellowish-white flowers: I had sampled one of the berries of the previous year.

Huge boulders littered the flanks of small hills. Flocks of bell-tinkling goats were carefully watched by seemingly

* See *John Hillaby's London*, Constable, 1987.

motionless old men and women leaning on crooks taller than themselves. What their animals fed on amidst that riot of scrub, I couldn't make out. And what were their minders thinking about, day after day, week after week? Could it be that they were not so much watching as *listening* for an occasional stray?

From behind the shelter of an old wall I looked back through glasses at a man who, as far as we could make out, hadn't moved for at least a quarter of an hour. A Vlach if ever I saw one. As I focused more intensely, the better to make out his rough coat and floppy hat, he turned round, looked in our direction and slowly raised his right hand. I felt almost certain we couldn't be seen. Was he employing some paranormal sense of watchfulness? Or was it that, even on the soft verge, the sound of our footsteps had suddenly stopped?

We wore floppy canvas hats ourselves, heavily peaked and nicely aerated with muslin on top. They were to prove the most useful objects bought *en route*. We pulled them down over our eyes and strode on, cautiously admitting that we were gaining momentum and that our packs were becoming at least tolerable.

Ahead of us rose the usual false crest pierced by a row of almost cylindrical peaks, rounded at the top like the heads of giants watching our approach. Slowly they rose higher and higher. What could they be? They resembled the plugs of volcanoes. I took a compass fix: near due west. Mount Helicon? Almost impossible. That massif some thirty miles away – as I knew from notes made in London – was composed of sandstones and shales folded on sedimentary limestones, nothing plutonic. The map, of course, told us virtually nothing. We were again conscious of moving in a fog of ignorance. What did it matter? Not for the first or the last time we clung to the light-hearted notion that we were invincible.

In a series of generous curves our good-mannered road
sauntered up to a small plateau beyond the crest. Up there
all appeared desolate, a rocky defile fit only for vultures and
brigandage. Cyclopean blocks of sandstone tinted bright
green and reddish-orange from algae and ferrous compounds
lay on top of each other in confusion, as if in some bygone
age a cathedral had collapsed.

Our road narrowed but never wavered. It knew what it
was about and inside a mile we were looking down on a
fertile and far-reaching plain chequered with smallholdings.
By some trick of perspective our volcanic plugs – if such
they were – seemed to have shifted some thirty degrees to
the north of our westering, but we couldn't make out
whether their phallic shapes stood above clouds of heat-haze
or behind another range, possibly far-distant Parnassus. We
never did find out and thereabouts we cared not at all for
we stood above the village of Melissohori at the chiming of
the Angelus. Pretty fair going, we thought, since we'd left
Thebes an hour after Prime.

The name of that village, perhaps only a hamlet – because
it appeared to have no purposive roads beyond the one that
led us there – enlarged our vocabulary by one golden word:
Melissohori, the resort of the bees, remembered thereafter
for a certain brand of golden lager* which, ingested under
heat and stress, has no fellow. It comes close to in-
defectibility, a liquid such as Athena pressed on Penelope
to ensure her constant affection. The name rolls over the
tongue. I can taste it now. Within three-quarters of an hour
– to the marked interest of the locals – we had emptied four
bottles. Par for our dehydrated course. A genial place.

Four very senior citizens in fustian dress sat alongside the
retsina bench addressing themselves to a common jug which
held about two litres. Two of them greeted us with a circular

* *Amstel*

hand wave, palm outwards and a muttered '*Yass*' short for *Yiasou*. Surprisingly no questions were asked about what we were up to but they were obviously fascinated by our packs parked against a whitewashed wall. Under pretext of studying our almost useless map we tried to correlate their vigorous sign-language with the few words we heard and understood.

The signs, which are probably older than proto-Greek if not sentient mankind, are mostly expressed with the right hand either clenched or with vigorous movements of the upraised or waggled index finger. In the terminology of music, the left hand may be regarded as *continuo* or figured bass, supplemented by engaging whirls of their worry beads. In serious argument, especially during backgammon, both hands are used vigorously, as in deaf and dumb or the tick-tack language of bookmakers.

The two who greeted us – we shall call them Pano and Stefano – were either trying to sell something, a mercantile matter, or else it had to do with village politics. They were as one with each other. '*Hronoi prin*,' – it had all happened before, one of them said, 'many years ago'. He confirmed the matter by raising his right palm and flicking it backwards as if throwing a coin over his shoulder.

The other two, let us say, Carlos and Joanni, were of a different opinion. Their spokesman, the one with a fearful scar over his eye, crossed his forefingers over his mouth and kissed them before letting out an explosive '*Ohi!* No! *Ma to Theo!*' which means 'By God! I'm telling the truth.'

About what? We never discovered. An old but agile *papas*, a priest entered the bar in a rustle of a somewhat superior brand of cloth. He turned to us and smiled as I stood up. '*Kalos orissate stin Melissohori*.' He was pleased to welcome us to his village. Would I please sit down. '*Kathise, parakalo*,' he said, extending his palm downwards and agitating his fingers as if patting an imaginary dog.

He greeted his parishioners, glanced into the wine jug, blessed it and helped himself to a modest measure. Glasses were raised: '*Kalee kairee.*' Thereafter they put their heads together, physically, and the argument resumed, loudly, passionately on the part of the laity. The priest spoke quietly, judiciously as if seeking approval for some disputed course of action. Eventually he sighed, shrugged his shoulders, picked up an empty cigarette packet and tore it open so that he could scribble on the black surface. Scribble *what*? A draft letter to their bishop? The odds on a horse at Corinth? How best to get another subsidy from Athens? Katie, ever charitable, suggested a Bible class or a meeting of the parish church council. Entering into the spirit of the occasion I whispered, '*Then andecho pia,*' I'm damned if I know. You can never be sure with a village *papas*.

Most of them are ill-educated and drawn from the ranks of the secular clergy. They are permitted to marry but on doing so forfeit all chance of preferment. With their often begrudged free meals, they tend to be regarded as a bit of a joke, as one of the village features together with the horse-dealer, the rural guard and the tavern keeper, but as man not as priest. Recall what we heard about those gun-toting clerics at Pili, on our second day out of Athens? Our *papas* could have been of their persuasion.

We were hungry. I stood up and put the matter to the priest as best I could. '*Papas, parakalo. May kovi lortha,*' and went through the motions of sawing my stomach in two. He smiled and shouted to someone downstairs to be answered by a subterranean and wholly incomprehensible screech. He pointed to a door behind two wine barrels and gave a thumbs down sign and a down-going motion with two fingers on his knee.

The stone stairs were as steep as hell and I felt like Orpheus in the Underworld. In a corner of the cellar a very old woman stood with her back to me, vigorously pumping air from leather bellows into the flowing ashes of a wood fire. There ensued an eruption of sparks in the manner of a firework remembered from youth as Golden Rain. She couldn't hear a thing I tried to say, and I climbed back to the parish council.

In a right paternal gesture the priest, his beard a foot from mine, put a hand on my shoulder and said, '*Danske?*' I shook my head and said, 'No, *ohi*, we are English,' and waved towards Katie. 'My wife,' I said. This appeared to please him and he nodded in her direction. Re-enter Scarface, left, puffing, slightly. Greeks who spend most of their time in taverns, like their English counterparts, get fat at forty. Some seem to have been born fat. Their active agrarian kinsfolk, especially meditative watchers of goats, for no metabolic reason I can think of are as skinny and tough as whips. To him that hath . . . Scarface had great news. He smacked his lips, noisily. '*Kotopoulo!*' To ensure there could be no misunderstanding he flapped his arms vigorously and vented that noise as Peter heard it, thrice.

I awoke very slowly. It seemed curiously dark. My newly purchased and much valued cap had slipped over my eyes. Katie lay beside me snoring, gently, her head on her prostrate rucksack. I could hear the melodious hum of bees. We had gone to sleep near three or four brightly painted blue, white and scarlet hives. I woke her up. 'Where are we?' she asked. I said I didn't know but could tell from the westering sun that we were alongside the little road that led towards our destination that night, the small township of Elopia.

We both stood up, somewhat unsteadily and tried to reconstruct what little we could recall. Katie remembered that the priest helped to put on her rucksack but it took two men, both laughing uproariously, to lift up mine, pretending they were saddling a horse. But what happened after that? I shook my head. 'Don't you remember the bridge?' she asked. 'You thought it would cool you off if you waded through the stream and I had to pull you back.'

I couldn't remember the stream but I had a hazy memory of a signpost pointing in the right direction. Had we paid our dues? Katie nodded. 'I did,' she said. 'You bought them another jug of wine and later they insisted we should drink with them, first retsina and then brandy. Huge ones, about a cupful. You drank half mine. That's what did it. I don't think we should go back to Melissohori on this trip. A pity. That old priest's eye opened and glowed when he spoke. Scarface had been to London. He was in the merchant navy.'

'He couldn't speak English, could he?' I asked anxiously. She shook her head. 'None of them could. I asked them in Greek and you gave them a short lesson in English which they seemed to like. They wrote some words down.' No comment on my part.

The time, nearly half-past four. As far as I could make out, we had walked for an hour after lunch, miraculously, and slept for an hour or thereabouts in the bee-loud glade, choosing a gentle depression carpeted with wild thyme in an orchard of old citrus trees. The marvel is that, apart from temporary amnesia and my sunburnt nose, we felt more energetic than we had any right to. Our packs were laid out, neatly; they were shouldered up and off we went, along a partly macadamized road with broad verges which were easy on the feet.

Almost everywhere, it seemed, we were in the company of bees. *Protinus aerii mellis coelestia dona exsequar . . .*

Let me sweeten my poem with honey for its theme, the
    gift of the sky.
Permit me now, Maecenas, to present for your
    entertainment a miniature state;

I will give you an account of its fierce-hearted leaders,
Its orderly tribes, their manners, their pursuits, their
  wars.
Is the subject too slight? Who will slight a poet's pains
If the gods do not grudge him and Apollo hears his call?

Thus the opening lines of Virgil's *Georgics*, Book IV, as translated and introduced by Robert Wells. Both in our heather-covered moorland garden and on many long walks together, Katie has patiently endured some of the forty or more lines from the *Georgics* remembered from school days. They were physically thrashed into me by an elderly Latinist who invited his favourite scholars into his bedroom study at the end of our dormitory. With unruly red hair, buck teeth and a marked tendency towards insolence, I wasn't among the chosen few. Although I've never had the slightest difficulty with binomials, the scientific names of plants and animals, especially insects, I hated that red-faced Glaswegian and some of us thought he had complicated the intricacies of Latin grammar and syntax to make our life almost intolerable.

One day I managed to buy a cheap second-hand parallel translation of the *Georgics*, probably a Loeb edition, and marvelled at the descriptions of animals I knew quite a lot about. 'First seek a settled home for your bees . . . place not their hives where the butting heifers can assault them. Let the spangled lizard with his scaly back be also a stranger to the rich stalls. Beware the bee-eater and Procne, the swallow with breast marked by bloodstained hands.'

Unfortunately I had picked up a very free translation and one, of course, well-known to the resident catamite of Vintner House, whose aberrations were as opaque to me as the pluperfect and the future perfect indicative active. With rasping irony he bade me unravel the meaning and syntax of the lines, word for word. More sadistic slaps on my bare backside after dark with a slipper. Since we were obliged to take a shower every night, I wondered why he was so concerned about the hygiene of my genitals. *O hominem impurum! Hey me infelicem!* The accusative of exclamation.

To go back to the evocative treasure in the work of Robert Wells: he says what Virgil seeks to do is to break his subject open, to till it and make it more fruitful. He wrote towards the end of devastating civil wars: 'Caesar against Pompey; Octavian and Antony against the murderers of Caesar; Octavian against Antony . . . Octavian promised an end to the guilt, a world no longer at odds with itself and a new peaceful beginning.' Virgil (70–19 BC) draws a parallel between his own nine-year-long struggle with the niceties of the *Georgics* – a word which means earth (*ge*) and work (*ergon*) – and that of the victorious Master of the Empire.

Notwithstanding the indiscretions of our lunchtime break Katie and I were knocking along at what we call a pretty fair lick, hugely encouraged by a signpost which promised that Elopia was no more than twelve kilometres away. The well-tilled soil intersected by irrigation canals and boundary-markers of pink and white oleander and dwarf cypress looked rich and humid enough to nourish crops of bananas.

With some time on our hands we throttled down to a modest pace, the better to take stock of veritable garlands of wild flowers. Some like fragrant jasmine and the electric-blue sepals of *lithospernum* made basket-work out of the stems of their taller sisters; others, especially a riot of orchids, most of which were entirely new to us, favoured the sloping but deep-cut banks of the water channels. We wondered who kept stock of the communal supply since, with a few greedy spadefuls taken out here and there, it would be an easy matter, we thought, to deplete the whole system.

By far the most charming aspect of the landscape was the integration of beekeeping with the density and variety of both the wild and cultivated flora. Most of the clusters of the three- and four-tiered hives reflected good husbandry, they were well cared for. Yet even in olive groves some errant swarms had built their clammy cells in natural fissures in the hard wood. The fissures had been either enlarged or cut away to provide the bees with landing platforms. Below these boughs, or around the parent trunks of the trees, thoughtful apiarists had put a necklet of chicken wire and thick cloth to protect their charges against spangled lizards and the like.

Virgil tells us how 'under the towers of Oebalia's citadel' – which is to say at Tarentum in Italian Calabria – he saw an old peasant 'who had a few acres of unclaimed land, a soil not rich enough for bullock's ploughing, unfitted for the flock and unkindly to the vine. Yet, as he planted herbs here and there among the bushes, with white lilies about and verlane and slender poppy, he matched in contentment the wealth of kings and, returning home in the late evening, would load his board with unbought dainties.'

T. E. Page remarks that 'to Virgil nature is not a dead thing but living and sentient. He constantly speaks of things as possessing almost human feeling.' This is echoed by Robert Wells who recalls Osip Mandelstam's trenchant line: 'We live deaf to the land beneath us.' Virgil had seen 'the empty fields running to waste' and 'the plough dishonoured'.

As we walked through the harmony of orchards, cereals, vegetables and vines tended with such care by labourers often working back to back, we thought about the inhuman, remorseless agriculture of depopulated areas of the Yorkshire Wolds and East Anglia. Did those get-rich-quick Euro-farmers ever set foot on their own land except to shoot game? Did they care a damn about other birds, bees, wild flowers, hedges, ditches and unpolluted streams? And yet . . .

According to the melancholic Robert Burton,' 'No rule is so general as that which admits of some exceptions.' A few marvels can be accomplished with next to nothing in the way of human effort. This came home to me hard on a long walk which ended at Nice.* After cresting the Bonette, that great pass on the fringe of the maritime Alps, all became downhill. The geometry is flowing and it flowed south, into *la grande chaleur* in the season of cicadas.

At St Auron or it may have been St Sauveur in the Gorges de Valabres, I settled down for one thrice-blessed night of luxury in a wayside tavern, almost exhausted. M. le patron, a sophisticated fellow, heard out my tale of where I had come from (Holland) with a marked lack of enthusiasm. 'Idleness', he said, 'is an appendix to nobility,' and to support this effrontery he told me how, many years before, he had been amongst the hard-drinking fishermen at Cannes. One of his fellows, a certain Auguste Célestin, retired to the hills where, from his mother, he had inherited a house, a little vineyard and one big *brusc*, a primitive beehive. Since Célestin knew nothing about hives or Virgil's philosophy a neighbour would extract the honey for him. Feckless Célestin never fed his bees, nor cleared the hive; never gave them water, never cut out the queen cells, never killed an old queen and never put in a new one. He did just nothing every year, and with no labour whatever he would be supplied with twelve to fifteen pounds of honey.

Another visitor, a fruit-grower from somewhere down the valley, listened to the story with marked interest. He shook his head. 'You are lucky', he said, 'that you had only one *fainéant* [drone] like M. Célestin.'

The twelve kilometres might be likened to an Irish mile or the length of a piece of string. Elopia, when we eventually got there, turned out to be a one-horse village. We saw the

---

* *Journey through Europe*, Constable, 1972.

horse, a skinny beast tethered to a tree in the *plateia*. Over an ouzo in a crowded bar we asked our host first where, *parakalo*, we could erect out little tent and, second, the lip-touching question about our interest in food.

He scratched his head, said something almost inaudible above the Niagara of noise of TV pop music and pointed through the window. Katie who had managed to catch a word or two said we were being invited to join the horse that night and that there was something in the kitchen. She sniffed. 'It's mutton,' she said.

Difficult to refuse both offers politely, though we were already fed up with mutton and were averse to sleeping in the local equivalent of Trafalgar Square. A customer with a smattering of English invited us to follow him. He lived at the back of the pub where with the pride of an estate owner he pointed to a concrete yard and then to his hen run, already tenanted by chickens on perches. Stalemate. More apologies on our part.

The outcome, briefly, was that one of a small band of really sympathetic youngsters led us to the spacious grounds of their locked-up schoolhouse where, after a word with the caretaker, with endearing enthusiasm they helped us to put up the tent under a huge cypress tree. As a bonus they pointed to a tap in an unlocked shed.

We reciprocated with lollipops all round from a very superior-looking *zaharoplastio*, the Greek equivalent of a *pâtisserie*, which unfortunately sold only coffee, sweets and delicious-looking sticky buns. The children waved, we waved and went back to the taverna.

Adequate rather than superior, but made memorable by the company and Katie's striking up a warm relationship with Mama Elena who was both the cook and the grandmother of the young boss – Aristotle, we imagine, but referred to by all the company as Ari. The place was packed. He pointed to two rickety stools at the bar and bade us wait there. Drinks? I resisted the idea of ouzo, feeling that after our over-indulgence earlier we ought to be reformed characters, so we ordered *krassi* (wine) *aspro* (white) *aretsinatos* (non-resinated). Katie is not over fond of retsina and in rural areas they usually serve it unless asked for something else.

Around us the sound of excited human voices fortified by electronic bouzouki bounced back from the crudely plastered walls and ceiling, and noise enveloped us. We were obliged to shout.

Before long Ari appeared from the kitchen and with the silent authority of a traffic cop waved Katie back there to order food, and me towards two empty chairs between two fat men at a table normally for six.

'What do you want?' Katie shouted.

'Best there is,' I shouted back, 'but no damned moussaka.' If overcooked it resembles dried-up shepherd's pie, the bane of my school dinners.

I couldn't decide whether my table companions were more interested in me or in our wine bottle. Perhaps both. All six, three men and three women, gave me a hearty welcome. '*Aspropato*', they shouted, which means 'White bottoms', the Greek equivalent of 'Bottoms up'. Six small glasses went up in the air, and three were banged down empty.

We went through the standard catechism and I gave very cautious answers – we had come from Thebes, we were going to Delphi, but I let slip the fact that we were on foot. Incredulous looks. I'm telling the truth, '*ma to Theo*' and I pointed to my dusty boots.

A few minutes before Katie returned I offered our bottle all round. It was seized upon by the menfolk for three brim-fillers and something close to a cheer. It became common property but they gestured vigorously towards their own almost full jugs. Much clashing of glasses and some apprehension on the part of this would-be penitent.

Greeks are among the most generous people in Europe but possibly through some inborn trading instinct they dispense their generosity in a ritualized manner. They are not to be taken for a ride. It's up to the stranger to make the first move. Thereafter they usually can't do too much for you. It came out later to our slight embarrassment that they were paying for everything we drank.

The company fell about when Katie appeared. Seats were rearranged so that she sat between me and one of their wives, a handsome well-dressed woman. A good arrangement since Katie has more than twice my grasp of linguistic essentials. She lifted her eyebrows at the sight of our almost empty bottle. 'Not me,' I said, defensively. 'I'll get another one.'

She shook her head. 'Make it a half,' she said. 'Remember Melissohori. Granny Elena is a darling, we got on fine. Grandson isn't married. She's a bit worried. You may have noticed he wears a ring through his ear.'

'But what about food?'

'The choise is between rather dry moussaka, an omelette or lamb stew, *arni kapana*. For *arni* read stringy mutton. Looks as if it's been simmering for days. We put our heads together. I found tomatoes, red peppers and aubergines which could be chopped up for a dressing. She seemed delighted, you'd have thought I'd just invented *boeuf Bourgignon*. Looks as if they'll all get it tonight.'

I introduced 'Katerina' and she met Toula, Thea, Antonio and Paris, each one accompanied by strange relationships we couldn't make out. A kiss for Katie, a hand-grasp and a mild thump on the chest for me.

Enter Ari and Granny proudly carrying a wooden stretcher bearing more wine and eight plates of *arni katerina*. Loud cheers. 'Looks like Brueghel's *Wedding Feast*,' whispered Katie. Granny made a little speech and pointed to her. More cheers. Clink, clink.

Underneath the lightly braised vegetables the mutton stew

tasted much as it does the length of the Balkans. The Greeks pride themselves on their cooking and say it has slowly evolved from Homeric feasts. Others say this is absolute nonsense, it's a mixture of Turkish and Italian dishes – despite the fact that there still exists in former Greek Sicily a temple dedicated to Adephagia, the Greek goddess of good eating and merriment. Perhaps under divine guidance she invented mutton stew.

A neighbour of ours, a much travelled architect and ecologist, claims that fundamentally there are only three ways of preparing local food: French, Indian and Chinese. But try explaining that to those whose culinary dream is of prime roast and Yorkshire pud, Thanksgiving turkey and apple pie like momma made, or even Hungarian goulash.

By feeble torchlight we circled the *plateia*, said goodnight to a farting horse, the first Elopian we had met, and took the wrong turning. A clear sight of the Plough and Polaris showed we were completely off course on a road back to Thebes. We turned round and saw the schoolhouse at the foot of a rustic track.

The tent looked inviting but we were far from alone. At our approach sparrows arose from a cypress and flew off with much twittering and whirling of wings. It sounded like distant applause. They circled overhead before settling on the schoolhouse and adjacent trees where the clamour died away except for a few birds which kept up a repeated *chur-tit-tit, chur-tit-tit*, the sparrows' alarm call.

Because the birds almost invariably assemble and fly in at dusk when their breeding season is over and done with, we could not have foreseen that we had camped out under a heavily populated roost. Unlike starlings which spend their nights on ledges in orderly lines, equally gregarious sparrows quarrel and tumble over each other in a confused mass, chirruping until they settle down. Roosts of up to 100,000 birds have been reported from several countries. Katie and I know vast assemblies on Hampstead Heath, and once in November we found that every tree in the fashionable Avenue Bourguiba in Tunis was so thickly covered that the tables for tourists had to be moved out of excremental range.

In Elopia we were tired and promptly slept until two in the morning when to our annoyance we were awakened by those damned birds. Above the twittering and excitement we could hear a musical *pee-oo, pee-oo* repeated softly at regular intervals for about twenty minutes. An owl, surely, but which owl? At dusk the next day we both heard and saw the slim little chap, Scops owl, only a few inches in height. The commotion died away and we slept again until the village awoke at the slow chiming of one bell. Prime in Ascension-tide.

We got away at a more civilized hour. It took time to wash our white-spotted tent under that invaluable tap. We packed up the better to enjoy a pint of strong tea with Granny Elena's parting gift, a packet of cheese and some fruit. All chores done, we strode along towards the distant flanks of Mount Helicon.

We were still on a narrowing plain of less rich soil, trimly laid out with lines of almond trees and olives interplanted with vines. Friendly labourers, always with covered heads and arms, greeted us with a loud '*Yass*', and waggled their mattocks and rakes, resting a while until we were out of sight.

Damned hard work, it seemed. Some more lines from the *Georgics* came back: *Multum adeo, rastris glaebas cui frangit inertis vimineasque* . . . 'Yea, and much service does he do the land who with mattock breaks up the sluggish clods . . . nor is it for nought that golden Ceres views him from high

Olympos with favour.' Presumably PASOK has laid down labour rates, but are they paid in outlying regions? Most of the workers were noticeably old folk. We guessed that their children and grandchildren were working in the cities.

By walking through the avenues of trees we could see more flowers than on the little road. Greece has a flora of at least 6,000 species, near twice the number to be found in Britain, wild bees including a huge blue creature were commonplace but relatively few domesticated species. Although we could hear the echoing *croomp* of men abroad with shotguns, the glades throbbed with birdsong. On most patches of waste ground we found at intervals of about a hundred paces the most vociferous of nightingales still deploring the violent adultery of Tereus and the fate of poor Itys. Many other birds are common, too: several different kinds of warblers whose songs could not be disentangled; the *chink* and stammer of tits and finches busy destroying fruit blossom; and the metallic rattle of rollers, sky-blue in flight and as large as jays.

And then a curious thing happened. All the glorious sound ceased. Not *tout à coup* but as if under electronic volume control – diminuendo, or cross-faded in studio jargon.

The sight of shotgunners? No! The birds had seen that fork-tailed predator the Black kite which swept across our path a few feet above the ground, buoyantly with long glides and slow wing-beats. It passed us almost overhead and the glorious sound was resumed.

On the road we came across the gunners dressed to kill: camouflage battle-dress, waisted with plaited leather belts to hold their twelve-bore shells and American-style peaked caps incongruously decorated with *tiroler* tufts of boar fur or pheasant feathers in the manner of the chorus from *The White Horse Inn*. Around their necks they carried silver or chromium-plated bird-callers which at intervals they *pou-*

poued like an amorous hoopoe, apparently to attract small doves, a specimen of which was carried by only one man, their sole triumph. I tried to ask about the Black kite, a species which I knew carried off farmyard chickens and goslings, and finished up by a makeshift imitation of the bird. I crouched and waggled my arms backwards but suspected from their serious expressions that they thought I wanted a toilet, since they pointed towards some bushes.

At hourly intervals, strictly speaking at twenty past the hour, church bells chimed. From behind us we could recognize, by a small crack in its voice, our own sanctuary away back in Elopia. It was echoed by an alto triplet *ping-pong-pang* from an unseen village in the hills to the south and, with increasing volume, a carillon pealed our due ahead. We had forgotten it was not only Sunday but that especially sacred one within the octave of Ascension-tide.

Half an hour passed. During a fine avian oratorio on all sides the bell-tower in front of us spoke plainly. The sound and its echo died away and, to our huge surprise, we heard, although at first faintly, a *kyrie* sung in plain chant with a stress *basso profundo* on the second line.

Kyrie, Kyrie
KYRIE ELEISON

Within an hour we stood outside the Church of Our Lady, the Panagia herself, a basilica of pink granite blocks under copper-green pendentives at the heart of the hamlet of Xironomi.

Groups outside as if at a synagogue on the morning of Sabbath – 'the cessation of labour' – greeted us like old friends. Without a head-shawl and wearing jeans, Katie felt she couldn't go in. I left her with a family dimly remembered from the night before, and entered a mystery: the service of the Orthodox Panagia, Mary the sanctified successor of the old Demeter transformed – Ceres of the Romans, protectress of man and of all the fruits of the earth.

The church was packed, the service somewhat confusing but the singing superb. Worshippers came and went, crossing themselves right to left, kissing one or more icons just inside the narthex. One very old lady, wholly in black, wept as she knelt before the stiff portrait of the Panagia; a good soul obliged to walk with a stick paused in front of an icon of the Last Judgement. She lowered her head, said a prayer audibly, and with a tremulous finger lightly touched a recumbent figure at the foot of the painting. After she had limped away I saw that she had touched the head of the Prince of Darkness, proud Lucifer cast down. I could make nothing of her simple gesture.

Orthodoxy has retained the basic simplicity of the earliest known churches. Only the priests and their deacons are permitted to walk behind the iconostasis, the high screen of icons which separates the sanctuary from the nave. The belief of this enormously popular and widespread religion is that Byzantine iconography excels realistic painting as a means to meditation. There are no statues within the church; they are reckoned to be impious relics of the polytheism of the pre-Christian era.

In between three hours of prayers and the reading of sacred literature there is much wholly unaccompanied chanting and singing, led by the clergy and by cantors of a vocal quality comparable only to that heard in High Anglican churches and cathedrals. I came out of the basilica strangely moved.

Katie had heard part of the service through the loudspeakers which had attracted us to the church. Better still, with a diplomacy which I wish I could emulate, she had approached several groups waiting outside and asked, politely, if they knew of anyone who spoke English. She introduced me to Georgios who had done his fifteen years overseas making and selling bread in the Bronx. He had interpreted part of the service for her although, as he put it, 'Shit! I haven't been on my knees since I left Xironomi.' He ran his father's farm nearby and drove his mother to church for the four great festivals.

I asked if he could explain the action of the old lady who had blessed the Devil. 'Don't know, but I'll ask Mamma when she gets off her knee-bending.'

With her twinkling eyes and ready smile, Ma was pretty spritely for her seventy years. He explained the situation rapidly. 'She don't know either,' he said. 'She don't go to church that often but she'll ask the old lady if you'll point her out.'

I saw her at once and nodded, and promptly regretted the action when I caught Katie's disapproving look. But too late, too late. The two old ladies were talking and, thank God, smiling. Apparently they were friends if not close neighbours.

Georgios' mother returned and with small gestures, as if she were blessing him, spoke benevolently. He translated, slowly. 'Mamma says Dora thought no one else seems to be praying for him and surely he needs prayers for forgiveness more than anyone else in the world.'

We felt peckish. Our friends left by car after giving us meticulous instructions about how to reach their favourite *kafenio* at the far side of the village, fortunately *en route*. Why couldn't they drop us there, he asked. Hard to explain that one briefly, but we knew the routine: we'd been going through it for nearly a week. We waved them goodbye, promising to mention their name to the *patron*.

Among the three or four locals was a fellow noisily slopping up yoghurt, a word which we couldn't pronounce easily (*yahourti*), but by saying who we had just seen and pointing politely we were given two generous portions topped by an inch of honey, the man behind the till pointing out his hives and the milk churns.

Katie stirred hers vigorously but paused over the last spoonful. She picked something off her tongue and handed it to me on her forefinger. 'What', she said, 'are these?' Two creatures the size of caraway seeds. Now as a Fellow of the Royal Entomological Society I knew damn well what they were: *aphodius*, a small dung beetle, which we shall shortly meet again. 'A tiny insect,' I said. 'They're common around here. They are probably good for you. Harmless.'

The man behind the till wouldn't take any money for our yoghurt, coffee and a packet of biscuits. 'Georgios,' he said with a theatrical wink, and on we went, on and on, during a long, long day which ended that night in a hell-deep gorge on Mount Helicon.

The countryside hilly, mixed agrarian and pastoral on progressively hillier slopes. The great range ahead looked ominous, a lop-sided massif with its left shoulder on our line of approach leaning south towards the invisible Gulf of Corinth. Few labourers about and fewer still when, on Georgios' advice, we struck right beyond a burnt-out church, at the old road – literally the *asprodhromos*, the white track. Up and up, in that fog of ignorance.

We rested, briefly, in the shadow of a shieling, the ruins of a house of somebody's grandfather. The huckling of hens, busy beehives and two open churns of milk wrapped about with moist rags, tomorrow's yoghurt under an old mulberry tree. We peered inside them. Many small insects, moths, flying ants and beetles, including *aphodius*, moved freely on the creamy surface of the milk.

'Is that what I nearly ate at lunchtime?' Katie asked.

'I think so,' I said, adding mendaciously, 'That's why

Boeotian yoghurt is so famous. It's another flavour, like banana or pineapple.' She didn't say any more.

The white track seemed to go on for ever.

As an abode of the gods Mount Helicon has been sung about for over 3,000 years. The Muses were reputed to have spent part of each year in a sanctuary up there. It lies behind Thespiae where there are the remains of a theatre, statues and an Ionic temple erected in their honour. Presumably the famous Nine used the place as a sort of shared holiday home. We wondered how Zeus and the rest of his improbable company got on at the top of so many feet of snow.

We have much of this in *The Theogony* or birth of the gods by Hesiod who, although born at Cyme in Aeolis, retreated, together with his unsuccessful father and his ambitious brother Perses, to the village of Ascra some miles to our north.

Hesiod, together with Homer from whom he probably borrowed extensively, sketched out the basic *Who's Who* of classical literature, but whence came this truly remarkable mythology? Simple answer: oral tradition, source wholly unknown. It still exists, or certainly did into this century.

More years ago than I care to remember, my brother Joe, an historian, and I crossed a little market-place near the superb Greek temple of Segesta near Palermo in west Sicily. According to Thucydides its ruins date from the third century BC. To an attentive audience of about a dozen villagers, a ragged old man who gestured with a thick baton was telling the history of the village in the tradition of the ancient 'mimes'. He spoke in a curious droning voice. He had got as far as the arrival of the Saracens in the ninth century when we arrived. By the time we returned about two hours later he was deep into the Pharos and the Knights of St John. My brother who has a fair grasp of Italian said that the narrator was pretty near the historical mark.

Wandering about in Attica and Boeotia somewhere around 750 BC is presumably how Hesiod acquired his extensive information whilst his brother wasted his patrimony and ultimately came to want. Hesiod relates how he lived the life of an industrious farmer (questionable) until the Muses met him as he was tending his sheep on Mount Helicon and taught him, like Caedmon of Whitby, 'a glorious song'. This was almost certainly the *Works and Days* and *The Theogony*. Glorious perhaps in showing from what meagre threads Homer wove the plumes and golden garments of his mighty armies. Hesiod's distinctive title to a high place in Greek literature lies in the very fact of his freedom from classic form and his serious yet child-like outlook upon the world. A near exact translation reads as though some amateur had tried to present Milton in the language of John Clare, the Northamptonshire peasant. Banalities abound.

> *Call your friend to a feast but leave your enemy alone and*
> *especially call him who lives near you . . . A bad neighbour*
> *is a great plague . . . not even an ox would die for him . . .*
> *Be friendly with the friendly and visit him who visits you . . .*
> *Do not let a flaunting woman coax and cozen. She is after*
> *your barn . . .*

Looking back I don't think we missed much in turning our backs on Ascra and Hesiod who in Quintilian's opinion 'rarely rises to great heights'. Even his name might be a literary twist on the Greek for 'the Guide'. As for his claim to have challenged and beaten Homer in a singing competition as related in the *Cypria*, I am at one with Jonathan Swift who, on the subject of classical poetry, wrote:

As learned commentators view
In Homer, more than Homer knew.

Herodotus maintained that Hesiod and Homer lived not more than 400 years before his own time, consequently not much before 850 BC. From his controversial tone it is evident that others had made Homer more ancient. What seems indisputable is that nobody knows when Homer actually lived.

The day seemed endless, the sunlight ferocious, the track confusing. We came across canals with steep concrete banks which we could see, from general bearings, wandered off in the wrong direction. We were very thirsty. We tried to fish for water by tying a length of cord to the neck of our plastic container – a precarious exercise. The water, when we managed to haul up about a pint, looked ominously discoloured.

We began to climb. We saw nobody except a shepherd too far away to be of any assistance. Katie sighed gently and murmured, '*Les choses . . .*' They were indeed *contre nous*. We tried to think of something to think about. The curious absence of bird life except those Crested larks. The heat haze. The horizons shimmered. Without saying a word I looked at them with mild consternation. They not only shimmered but a portion of a crest far away to the north appeared to detach itself from the general lie of the land. A mirage? *Le cafard?* Or perhaps, far worse, the onset of hyperthermia, heat exhaustion? The Psalmist's sickness that destroyeth in the noon-day. I had encountered it in the desert, often. We needed salt. We carried salt tablets but without water they bite. We had to find at least a cupful.

Under various pretences I probed every steep gully, overturned large stones for a glimpse of moisture. God be praised we found a freshet, a mere trickle but with the addition of two saccharin-sized tablets it tasted like iced Bollinger. A metabolic explosion. We pressed on.

About an hour later we entered another low defile where the tracks divided as decisively as the Y-forked hazel twig of a water diviner. Should we go right or left?

'Packs off,' I said. 'You go left and I'll go right. It'll only take us a few minutes to see what's ahead.' I had a notion that I was literally right.

I hadn't got half-way up my slope when Katie gave a great shout: '*Thalatta! Thalatta!*' The sea! The sea!

Stumbling up to her with both packs I saw the Gulf of Corinth stretching into infinity. In the blazing white sunshine it was wrinkled like beaten pewter.

Coastal Encounters

With scarcely enough water left to brew a mugful of tea we took to the shade of another ruined farmhouse which, to judge from concrete apertures and walls pock-marked by spent bullets, had been used as a military strongpoint. Inside it felt pretty warm but tolerable. Leaving Katie to make a temporary divan out of sleeping-bags on a fallen door propped up with bricks, I made for a rift, a depression in the slope of Helicon marked by a Golgotha of pink-flowered Judas trees.

Flood debris at their feet still felt moist. Like a questing hound I moved down the depression, first to a sprinkling of iris and asphodel where I thought I heard the belch of frogs. O blessed sight! A reed-ringed pool of clear water over which flew electric-blue dragonflies! I half-filled our plastic carrier, screwed it tight and returned to Katie claiming I had found the Fountain of Hippocrene. She seemed, I thought, singularly unimpressed. Whilst the butane burner hissed I scanned the landscape through glasses from the Gulf below us up to the highest peak of the range above.

On the map the coastline of the Gulf of Corinth thereabouts has a somewhat dissipated appearance beset by small bays and long wedge-shaped promontories which hang down like the dugs of a nanny-goat. In our constant efforts to cling to hard-won altitude they were to be avoided at all costs. But surely only one bay could boast of three small islands – the Dombrenis group – and there they were, due south, about a mile in length and twice that distance offshore. Surely even Greek maps couldn't be off-course by a day's march? The peak to the west of Ascra must be Motsara where Hesiod claimed to have received divine inspiration from the Muses, those nubile immortals who danced round their swimming-pool, Hippocrene. Maybe I wasn't all that far out in saying where the solvent of our tea had come from. This stuff, said I, taking immoderate gulps, contains the very essence of inspiration.

For the first time since we left Elopia with its bees, its hospitality and the field of the farting horse, we knew precisely where we had got to. How to get to Prodromos, the next place in the right direction on our miserable map, was still covered in question marks. We were surrounded by that ubiquitous prickly stuff.

An old but vigorous fellow seemed anxious to help but was busy trying, unsuccessfully, to control a herd of anarchic goats with blasphemous shrieks. Apparently he hadn't heard of Prodromos – rural Greek villages often changed their names during the Civil War. But at the word *paleohoro*, the old village, and a wave towards the north-west, he resorted to vigorous sign-language. Up there, on to the hill and then down, down steeply towards the left.

Relatively easy, until we got to the boulder-strewn summit of the hill he'd indicated where tracks wandered off in various direction but not the one we wanted.

Then very faintly, from afar, we heard the familiar, the dreadful noise that donkeys make when they imagine themselves unloved. Within half an hour we reached the tavern in the steep hill village of Prodromos.

Almost nobody about. What on earth were they all up to? Except for a muttered '*Yiasou*' in the tavern, little sound but grunts, the triumphant slap of a winning card and the rattle of boxed dice. We were so accustomed to being greeted loudly and promptly cross-examined that we felt obliged to speak in whispers.

No matter. We had found what had been on our minds for some hours: ice-cold Amstel beer which we drank outside in the company of an old dog who scratched himself excessively. Somebody observed that fleas are good for a dog: they stop him from brooding over being a dog. The atmosphere intrigued us. We sensed tension, waiting, as for a solemn thing about to happen. It began with the slow, the distant tolling of a bell. The old men inside rose to their feet and stayed there holding their caps in both hands. The man of the house came out pulling on his jacket. He shouted at the dog as a cortège climbed the hill. We inclined our heads as the procession approached.

First four priests, their lips moving in inaudible prayer, then the black-sashed bearer of a huge cross inlaid with silver. Then a battered van with an open coffin protruding from the tailboard. Inside could be seen half-shrouded shoulders and bare head of a very old man, his mouth agape as if in an arrested scream, fearful to look at. Then followed a long trail of relatives and other mourners, perhaps the whole village. They passed out of sight round a bend of the road. We sat down. We were alone in the forecourt except for the dog which had slunk back.

Half an hour elapsed before the whole company returned in a far from funereal mood. Certainly two or three women wept quietly, but they were kissed and hugged. Jugs of wine and little glasses of liquor on trays were handed round. A young man came up and in flawless English said: 'My name is Spiro. Momma thanks you for your respect. Will you please take a drink with us?' Saying that he would be back in a moment he returned to the company who were intent on exorcizing the stark fact of death with secular festivities:

upraised glasses. With hands round each others' shoulders they talked as if at a wedding. The tops of tables were wet with wine. A bouzouki combo struck up. Mock fights broke out and ended quickly with much back-slapping. All part of the ambiguities of Hellenism: violence and compassion, a capacity for survival and an ability to see things as they really are.

As our new friend Thomas Spiro, a well-to-do Cretan put it: 'This is how we are all going to end up, so we might as well have a good time at the rehearsals.' He said that the dead man was an old-guard Marxist and had probably left a small fortune. 'That's practical politics. During the Occupation he took most of the village up into shacks on Helicon where he lost an arm during raids. For the last twenty years he damn well ran this place. Anybody who stood up to him got chucked out or a warning shot in the leg. Pity he can't see what's going on now. *Endaxi*, eh? All kiss and make up, but in a few days' time they'll be at each others' throats again. To hell with it. We'll be back in Iraklion.'

As to our roundabout route to Delphi via Kirra and the Sacred Way, he couldn't understand why we didn't take the direct route through the hills to Distoma; we'd be there in half the time. We tried to explain. He shrugged and lifted his glass saying, 'White bottom.' I lifted my own and said, '*Aspro-pato* and thank you, all of you. Our blessings on your house, may it stand forever.' He bowed to Katie. His huge moustache brushed my cheek. We waved to the company, they shouted back cheerfully, and once more we were off again.

What had he said? Skirt the back of the village through their vineyard. Ignore the road. Keep to the track until we could see the sea and one small island. Look out for an old signpost that pointed up a track to the monastery, a steep hill but it could be trusted. He had known the place since he had worn short pants.

No doubts, no misgivings until, feeling tired out, we came to the hill. It wasn't a hill, it was a stony goat track up a steep cliff. We puffed and grunted. Hard going.

On the hill of the Holy Brethren we found the stream Spiro told us about. The last there was, he'd warned us. Musical water that tasted like Perrier. We filled up a stoppered plastic udder – enough for supper, a catlick wash, and breakfast. Near two litres. Heavy even when half full, and we were still trudging up and up to a steep rocky defile that twice echoed this uncertain path-finder's shout down to Katie.

'Enough,' she shouted back, 'let's stop here.' 'Here,' said the echo. '*Here*,' whispered another. I agreed with them. We'd stop, but where? The perennial, the ever-to-be-faced problem at sundown: where to doss down in that riot of rocks, thorns and tares entangled? Why the Desert Fathers sought holiness and hardships in Lower Egypt I could never make out: by comparison with what we were up against in the ruins of Arcadia, sand would have been luxurious, and mere pebbles tolerable.

With a womanly eye to exterior decoration Katie homed in on a large pink-flowered Cistus, high-arched enough to be crawled under. 'Roses round the door,' she said, not noticing, I suspect, that at the back a rounded lump of limestone stuck out like a partly submerged porpoise.

'Not quite our place,' I said, but quickly added that if she sat down I'd scout around on my own. She looked tired. Eventually we settled for a hollow in a bank which smelt of wild thyme and could, with imagination, be described as mossy. Behind it an aromatic herb, probably rosemary, symbol of fidelity. Newly-weds used to roll on it.

With tent up, supper on the boil and a shot of Metaxas as an aperitif we felt we could relax. A small prick-eared owl greeted us with a gentle *pee-oo* (pause) *pee-oo* before floating off on fairy wings.

115

Katie began to lay out supper of reconstituted Turkey Creole – whatever that is – but in a necklet of chopped-up walnuts and figs it went down all right. We lolled back with our heads on our packs recalling incidents of a day that had begun well and ended not too badly.

To ensure that we knew where we were heading for the next day I replayed my recorded instructions about how to reach the monastery. For a minute or two Spiro's voice came through loud and clear, and the sequence ended in fond farewells and sounds of revelry at the end of that tape. I turned it over and put the little machine away.

As a dog stands up and turns round before it settles down for the night I suggested we should wander round for a few minutes in the almost dark. Far below, pewtered in the unearthly light, we caught a glimpse of the cold and ancient gristle of the sea. The moon sailed through a sea of wrack. As the lightest of cat's-paw winds shifted a little to the east and then counterwise to the west the warm air bore the aroma of all-abundant honeysuckle and oleander. Faintly, far away from somewhere in the depths of the gorge a nightingale jug-jugged and chirruped at intervals, hesitantly as a concert flautist might moisten his lips and play a few bars before the conductor raises his baton. Its song cannot be reduced to the phonetics of bird watchers. Izaak Walton caught the spirit of it: 'Such sweet loud music they breathe that it maketh mankind to think that miracles are not ceased.'

Suddenly we seemed to hear music, vaguely familiar. Was there witchery abroad, such as Falstaff heard in Windsor Forest at midnight? With mock-severity Spiro had warned us that in that gorge, despite the proximity of the holy brethren, there were *daoutis*, evil spirits. The music grew louder. As we approached the tent we recognized Stravinsky's *The Rite of Spring*. The wild Bacchanale before the sacrifice of the maiden. Hypnotic percussion from the bass viols. In our minds' eye we could see the *corps de ballet*, those knock-kneed Lolitas with long braided hair.

The music came from my micro-recorder: in putting it away apparently I'd turned it on again. Until I spooled the tape back I couldn't understand why we hadn't heard the music before we took our stroll. Then all became comprehensible: a silence of about three or four minutes before part of one movement of the Stravinsky began. The recording was part of a series of hour-long BBC programmes called 'Man of Action' in which a few of us such as walkers, solo yachtsmen, mountain climbers and glider pilots were asked to select music that ran through our heads in moments of exhilaration and stress. The tape, an old one, sounded tinny but it meant we were carrying a little less than an hour's private concert with us. We spooled on and settled down to the harmony of violins in the final diminuendo of Mozart's 'Ave Verum Corpus'.

That darned nightingale turned up again after midnight, this time about twenty yards below us, where it encountered invincible rivals, the echoes in the gorge of its own voice. In vain it chattered and trilled until it flew away, whimpering. But a resolute nightingale: it came back twice during the night when, heartily tired of rolling over on top of each other, we got up and re-aligned our sleeping-bag so that on the slope we were able to rest feet downwards.

An hour before dawn we heard the whinny of a horse, the bleat of sheep and goats and the bark of dogs on the track below our shelf. Who were they? Vlachs? We hoped we couldn't be seen. At first light we could still hear the dogs at a distance and decided to pack up soon, leaving breakfast until we reached the elusive monastery. As a dog deterrent I whittled down a gnarled branch of a Judas tree with my skinning knife for as effective a shillelagh as ever you saw.

Before we set off I fished out a couple of sheets of Vlach

expressions from the fellow we had met on the train. On a small hilltop overlooking the plain we spotted a piratical-looking rider on a fine grey. He wore a dark goatskin cape surmounted, arrogantly, by a bright red knitted sock.

Leaving Katie I walked towards him slowly. Two or three lean curs bounded up, aggressively. He reduced them to belly-crawling submission by terrific shouts. Leigh Fermor says that, from shouting to each other across the windy tops of their hills, Vlachs are almost incapable of quiet speech in the open air. He watched my approach with contrived indifference. A middle-aged fellow but heavily bearded, an adornment which, apart from those on priests, is relatively rare in Greece. Red-sock bore a rich growth in which a pair of sparrows could have nested. Holding up my arms in greeting I bawled '*Yass*'. He shouted something similar and spurred his nag towards me. In basic Greek I said my wife and I were English; we were walking down to Kirra on the Gulf; where, please, is the monastery? There followed something in gruff speech and sign language I couldn't understand. I tried a different tack: '*Bunâ dzua! Dukesku! Paree Kalo Z'burask. Eshti Vlachos?*' At that fragment of Wallachian he smiled hugely, dropped his reins and with hands on pommel vaulted to the ground in one acrobatic movement.

'*Bunâ dzua!*' he said with evident satisfaction. Seeing comes before words. The child looks and recognizes before it can speak. There is what Dylan Thomas called an international flavour in most if not all European languages but Red-sock and I didn't get very far in terms of verbal communication.

He was a Vlach called Janos; I was an Englishmen Yanni, married (*hiu sura*) and there she was, I said, pointing to my bed-mate (*mulliari*) Katerina under a tree. I waved, she waved, he waved. To her I held my arms out laterally as if about to fly which, in our sign language, means, 'I'm fine.

Stay where you are.' Thereafter only two things I learnt, one distinctly negative: I couldn't put across where we were heading for. I tried *monastiera* and *basiliki*. He looked puzzled. I put the tips of my fingers together in the manner of the Hindu greeting. I crossed myself, looked up at the sky and murmured *papas*. He shook his head. Perhaps he thought we weren't too sure about the weather.

After scratching his head he pointed to the hills to the north and said something out of which I managed to abstract only one word: *Arachova*. The village on the main road between Livadia and Delphi.

I smiled hugely and said, '*Graz, graz,*' thank you but no! '*Nu, nu. Pou ine Antikira?*' Where was that little port on the Gulf?

His turn to look pleased. He swung his arm round, first to the south and then to the west. '*Ashits, ashits. Dukesku Antikira.*' Yes, yes he knew the place.

With a glance at my notes on Wallachian I could have told him that his dog (*canili*) was barking (*alatra*) and the house (*casa*) was old (*easti veacli*) but without them my vocabulary was limited to about twenty memorized phrases and incantatory words such as numerals and the present, past and future tenses of the verbs 'to be' and 'to have'. Not the stuff of intimacy. Two men (*doi barbata*) on donkeys (*gumari*) were working their way up to us driving their sheep and goats. Time to go, but Janos wouldn't have it. He asked me, as they all did, how old I was. This threw me. I knew only the words from one (*un*) to ten (*tsats*). Slowly I lifted up my open-fingered hands seven (*shapte*) times. He started and said something incomprehensible. Did it mean 'What a splendid fellow' or 'Silly old sod'? I shall never know. As far as I could make out from similar gestures on his part he was about thirty-five. He gripped my shoulders. We said '*Mulza ardio*' several times and I made my way back to Katie who, with her head on her rucksack and eyes closed, was

119

enjoying what the travel packagers sell to uncritical indolents as the joys of the Mediterranean littoral.

'Were they really Vlachs? What did you say to him?'

'Precious little. As far as I could make out he didn't know much Greek and I couldn't remember Vlach phrases until I glanced at my prompt.'

'Where are we heading for?'

'Back to the sea, I'm afraid. He indicated there's a track there to Antikira.'

'Why there?'

'It's near Kirra. Old Red-sock had actually heard of the place and it's marked on the map.'

Down we went, on to a small road where, hidden among trees, we found two trucks, the rear doors webbed with knotted rope. One looked like a very old army vehicle crudely camouflaged in a mosaic of dark green, brown and sickly yellow paint; the other was covered in faintly blue threadbare canvas. The trucks were double-deckers. There were two floors, one above the other and both were inches deep in sheep and goat droppings. Fresh donkey dung fouled the tailboard to which, presumably, the beasts were strapped in transit. So this is how they travelled at night from one grazing ground to another, the Black Departers. We had twice seen small convoys of similar trucks very early in the morning, and had assumed they were farmers taking their stock to market.

With his usual lucidity Patrick Leigh Fermor says; 'Ordinary Greeks approve of their [Vlachs'] Greekness, their freedom, admire their primeval severity of life but despise their primitive ways. "They never wash," they say, "from the day of their birth till the day of their death." Their aloofness promotes distrust. Plainsmen speculate about their buried and suppositious wealth. They regard them as sly opponents and the two are often at loggerheads when nomad flocks encroach on their grazing ground.'

Later on, in the Agrapha Mountains, those hostile peaks to the north-west, we found that the Vlachs were the only temporary inhabitants to practise transhumation, the custom of driving flocks up into pockets of high grazing-ground in the burning heat of summer and returning to hutments on the plains before inhospitable winter set in.

To reach the coast we took to the banks of a canal which appeared to run parallel to the line of the shore, and had to abandon it when it veered inland. The going became steep: a goat track down through a landslide of rocks. It led us to an almost deserted fishing village unmarked on our map but remarkable for the carcases of caiques and a ramshackle tavern supported on the seaward side by wave-worn stilts.

The company of four included a Master Mariner who knew precisely where he was and what we might expect when we again ventured inland. The man of the house served us with Amstel, bread and hot mutton broth, and in between mouthfuls we were again thoroughly examined.

At the question: 'Where have you come from?' we produced our maps, easier than explanations. The Master spoke with authority: '*Alla tara poro simera?*' – Where next today? I shrugged my shoulders. If I could have put across the irony in Greek I would have said: 'We have nowhere to go but everywhere.' I pointed to Antikira on Sheet 2, *Nomos Phokis*. He clicked his tongue. '*Simera?*' A long way, he said, about twenty-five kilometres. He picked the map up, holding one corner between two fingers as one might the tail of a rotting fish. We knew just what he felt. We were bidden to wait.

Within minutes he came back wearing a navy-blue cap with threads of gold around the peak. On the table he spread out the equivalent of an Admiralty chart with a section of the coastline. 'You are here,' he said, stabbing a small appendix to the Bay of Zaltsas with his forefinger. Their own village, Panagia, lay a little to the west.

Briefly the fog of ignorance was dispersed. But to Antikira there were neither paths nor small roads that we could make out, unless we went back on our tracks and up to Arachova.

The Master took my sheet and drew a decisive line up into the nearby hills, an *asprodhromos*, a white road, a very ancient track, the one they used during the war. Within an hour we were up and away, climbing steadily through hamlets with names.

Unlike our helter-skelter down the goat trail, the upland track rarely rose or fell with anything that irregulated a steady pace. It bore the spirit of antiquity, a purposive ongoing quality, a gradual ascent that followed contours and old terraces near the very end of their productive tenure, and we blessed the Master who had pointed it out.

On a staircase of ruined terraces we heard fearful screams. In a state of manic fury an old man thrashed the bloodstained flanks of a donkey in his efforts to drive the iron shoe of his plough into a forty-five degree slope. The flayed beast, with a fearfully visible cage of ribs, stumbled and fell to its knees. The old fellow stopped for a moment to prise out a large rock before he resumed his screaming and thrashing. Sisyphean labour. To what end? To hack out a path or a springwater channel from the small carpet of greenery above him, perhaps his sole holding in that wilderness. It seemed hopeless, the last despairing gesture of husbandry at the end of its tether.

Perhaps not entirely hopeless. On the highest slopes, within the shadow of the Helicon ridge, stood herdsmen as immobile figures, each with his own wardship. From our ongoing track we tried to pace out their small patches: a linear mile or less. They depended on skindeep soil, barely capable of sustaining and providing anchorage for goats' fodder. The question remained: What on earth were those silent wardens thinking about?

Towards sundown we faced up to finding water and somewhere to bed down with less than Spartan rigour. Doubt about the merits or otherwise of an inexplicable platform of fractured concrete in a depression were resolved by leaving our rucksacks there and setting off on our own to look for more comfortable lodgings.

I gave up within five minutes and rejoined Katie on the platform to find our packs beset by columns of small red ants which bit us painfully when we brushed them off. She had found what was probably a holiday home of a rich Theban merchant. Apart from the superb view across the Gulf, we couldn't make out why anybody had built a modern bungalow in almost complete isolation except for a track down to a small bay. We knocked on the door. Somebody shouted what presumably meant, 'Who's there?' Katie shouted back, 'Good evening. We are on foot. We need water. Can you help us?'

A bearded middle-aged man with dark, deep-set eyes appeared from the patio on the seaward side of the bungalow. He nodded, sympathetically and said something we couldn't understand but he lifted up his finger which we took to mean that we should wait. We heard him talking to a woman, rapidly and in a language we guessed was Serbo-Croat, then they came out together, smiling somewhat fixed smiles: she, a gypsy-like woman whose nervous eyes never left ours. We were shown the water tap and invited to take a drink with them on the patio. Then there began one of the most puzzling and intriguing hours we ever spent under a Greek roof.

★　★　★

The only verbal communication was between Katie and the woman of the house, whose Greek was only a little better than her own. The couple were hospitable. Eventually they gave us, two complete strangers, a meal and offered us a bed in a small room, but they were suspicious of every move we made to the extent of standing outside the lavatory door until we emerged. The man, Karol, watched me closely when I took off my jacket and shirt and washed in the kitchen sink. Both he and his companion Magda treated Katie in the same way. These moves were embarrassing but we couldn't do anything about it. What were they so concerned about?

Karol and I passed the partly open door of a room lined with books. He closed the door a little too quickly for decorum, but not before I caught a glimpse of the deck of a modern radio transmitter. From hooks alongside their double-bolted door hung a canvas game-bag, very curious leather straps, a holster and a bandolier for shotgun ammunition. Alongside on a shelf were boxes of twelve-bore cartridges and small taped-up cartons labelled Biretta 9 mm. So that's what he carried in that under-arm harness.

Shotguns are for sport but with a 9 millimetre slug you could blow a hole through a church door. I felt mildly alarmed. Why on earth had they let us in? If we could have got out under some pretext, Katie would have been the first through their bolted front door, but try as I did, I couldn't speak to her privately.

Tension is contagious. Choosing a deep chair on the patio, Katie all but sat on a very superior cat, a Burmese which became air-borne. At its howl I rose to my feet apologetically and knocked over a carafe of wine, which did nothing to improve the situation. Supper, a good supper, was served and eaten punctuated by polite platitudes between Magda and Katie. In an effort to bring a little warmth to the table, she talked of our home in *Londino*, our children, and our travels in Greece. Then, '*Apo pou ine?*' Where did they come from, she asked conversationally. The question seemed to freeze in mid-air. A short silence before Magda spoke rapidly in their own language, and then in Greek translated what Karol replied. Katie turned to me. 'She says that like ourselves they travel a great deal.'

'What next?' I asked with an expansive and wholly hypocritical smile. 'We are going to bed as soon as we decently can,' she said.

We slept for nine hours and were up and away by seven o'clock. Our hosts gave the impression that they hadn't been to bed.

By following the line pencilled on our map by the Master it took us two days of hard slog to reach the foot of the Sacred Way. It entailed climbing up the seaward face of Mount Helicon and – almost certainly in error – climbing down again through a steep boulder-strewn gorge. This put us back, painfully, for half a day. But there were compensations, especially the folk we met who were as helpful and straightforward as the two of the previous night had been mysteriously suspicious about everything we did. Even their external gear abounded in question marks. Surely a couple with intricate aerials and a powerful spotlight on the flat roof of a bungalow wouldn't get far as secret agents?

We didn't discover until we replayed all our micro-recordings several weeks later that the curious incidents we discussed *sotto voce* in our hosts' bedroom were irregularly overlaid and sometimes obliterated by electronic noise.

At midday we stared with no enthusiasm across a barren plateau bounded to the north and a little to the west by the snow-clad summits of Helicon and Mount Parnassus. On that plateau the old road split into a variety of tracks, as if uncertain where to go next, so we made for a distant procession of power pylons. Each of the nearest three was inhabited some half-way up by an amiable villain doing something to the metalwork. The first fellow seemed hugely amused by our arrival. He waved, he shouted something to his mate on the ground in the language we had heard the night before: staccato consonants and deep-throated auxiliary vowels as in *Brezhnev*.

I looked up and shouted: '*Parakalo. Theloome to voeethema.*' We needed his help, a phrase at which I had become adept.

'*Angleekee?*' he asked. I nodded. He called to the man on the other side of the pylon. In the manner of a character from Damon Runyon he asked 'Whad'ya want?'

'The old track down to Antikira,' I said.

'Jesus! If ya wanna kill yourselves, climb that hill and make for the shack you can see from the top. Mama Anoula's place. She'll make ya coffee. Don't reach for ya pocket or she'll go bananas. Say you're friends of Gregor's. Ask her to point out the Devil's Arse (*kolos too thiavolo*), a river bed. It's dry now but filled with goddam rocks. It'll bring you to the bauxite plant at a shit-heap called Paralia; there's a road from there to Antikira.'

'You from round here?' I asked.

'Us? Jeez no! *Voulgarous*, Bulgarians. I mean we wuz before the bastards started to shoot each other. Now we're Greeks. No goddammed work in Sofia. We come here by truck from Livadia each day.'

We did what he suggested. Impossible to guess Mama Anoula's age. A very active old lady, her skin wrinkled but her eyes bright and shining. She took Katie's hand as if her favourite grandchild had come home. After driving out a flock of indignant fowls she dragged us into her wooden hut with its iron stove and an array of pots for making cheese. Coffee? Impossible to refuse. She was grinding the beans. We drank it on a bench outside. We talked awhile, mostly murmuring pleasantries, then, leaving to Katie the problem of how to reach the *kolos too thiavolo*, I walked round the small-holding with map and compass, peering down, trying to work out where we'd got to. Discouraging. Several tracks disappeared in the shimmer of heat. We had strayed off the Master's line.

Katie called, 'Time to be off. Granny says it'll take us about an hour to reach the gorge.' Fond farewells, embraces and off we went.

Within ten minutes an eagle-like shriek pulled us up. Far back we could just make out Granny bounding down towards us with the agility of a goat. She stopped and pointed decisively with her right arm. We were on the wrong track. We swung to the right, she urged us on with upward movement of both arms. We found a much wider track. Apparently satisfied, Granny waved and trudged back. A wonderful old lady. She had given us abounding affection, coffee, and before we left she wrapped up a huge piece of feta cheese which we nibbled for days.

Soon afterwards I discovered that on my short foray alone I had lost a map, a compass and my snap-on sunglasses. The first two didn't matter; we were close to the next map sheet and, as usual, a small spare compass had been sewn into the pocket of Katie's rucksack. But my eyes ached from the westering sun.

Despite what Gregor said about the Devil's Arse, it didn't look particularly difficult: silvery sand between rounded slopes. A meandering but, as we were to discover, a very deceptive gorge. Within half a mile our complacency evaporated. Beyond the first right-angled bend we came to the ruins of a massive land-slip which had all but blocked the defile. From there the going worsened to a point where I wondered whether we should be able to get through without trying some real mountaineering. The slopes became cliffs with here and there an ominous overhang. The gorge narrowed, the stones became a torrent of boulders and in scrambling around them we sweated profusely.

At the appearance of yet another bend I left Katie to rest in the shade whilst I rounded the thing, hoping at best for a sight of the sea below. At worst I could judge whether we could get through slowly, with care. Instead I found a promising length of gravel. At this I tootled merrily on my whistle *staccatissimo*.

At critical points our packs tended to throw us off balance. The air became hotter and more still. I made vulgar jokes about the nether anatomy of His Unholiness. I contended, imaginatively, that we'd already got through the worst half of the whole damned cave.

'What cave?' Katie asked, looking up at the narrow band of skylight.

'This one,' I said. 'When the great ice melted thousands of years ago the plateau below Granny's place bècame the shoreline of a huge lake not far from the sea. Remember that silvery sand? The water rose higher and higher. The side pressures must have been enormous. The lake burst through the walls of the cave and brought the roof down. These rocks have been polished by ancient cataracts, not seasonal rains.'

Katie has become accustomed to Sermons on the Mount. 'But what's that,' she asked, 'a volcano?' – pointing to a plume of smoke rising from behind yet another bend. I didn't know.

Forgetting what the Bulgarians had told us, we were surprised to look down on the enormous bauxite plant at Paralia on the Gulf of Antikira. After the hours of eerie silence in the gorge we were taken aback by the squalor and noise. Workmen were excavating with pneumatic drills and pile-drivers. Among fuel stores, dumps and railyards bells clanged and small engines whistled as they shunted trucks of grey-white clay into the furnace sheds. Activity on all sides.

Threading our way through the debris we made for a harbour of sorts and settled down at the foot of a blockhouse heavily protected by barbed wire. Notices said we were in danger of death from high explosives. Pretty soon we had rehydrated and then boiled the contents of two packets of Caribbean Sweet Beef with Chillies, accompanied by a pint of coffee as a poor substitute for that Greek elixir of life, Amstel. Nutritious as it probably was, after several spoonsful of the unappetizing mess I decided to award the *Cordon Noir* to Dr Sydney Schwartz, one of the prime begetters of these dehydrated foodstuffs designed originally for astronauts and then mountaineers and long-distance walkers. That assassin of good food, a scientist in the pay of the US Space Agency, went one better and devised what he had the impertinence to call 'edible structural material'. This meant that after take-off the dispensable parts of a man-carrying rocket could be eaten by those prepared to tolerate the ultimate in gastronomic crime.

'More coffee, please,' I said. 'At least it takes the taste away.'

'Hold it,' said Katie. 'Here comes Nemesis.'

A camouflage-painted jeep bounced down towards us. It stopped. An elderly man stepped out, locked the door and approached with the swinging gait of a guardsman. A shrewd fellow with a clipped moustache, and cornflower-blue eyes under a semi-military kepi. He wore a tight-buttoned jacket notable for a little gold ribbon on the collar.

He stopped, saluted and said in clipped French, '*Monsieur et madame, Lieutenant Perouse, Chef de Sécurité, Vos cartes, s'il vous plaît.*'

He went through our travel-worn passports page by page, pausing over the stamps, Tunisia, Morocco, France, Cyprus and Russia – '*Pourquoi avez-vous visité la Russie?*'

We were travellers, I told him, interested in seeing as much of the world as we could, on foot. Experience has taught me that admissions about being an author or, worse still, a journalist are distinctly unwise in the presence of officialdom.

'So you are British, *monsieur et madame?*'

Almost imperceptibly his shoulders stiffened. *'Moi, je suis Légionnaire.'* With pride he held out his own discharge: *'Lt. Ramond Perouse, Régiment de Marche de la Légion Étrangère, Sidi bel Abbes, Algérie, 1962.'*

'But, monsieur, Algeria gained its independence that year.'

'That is true,' he said. 'We blew up our barracks in Zeralda and were allowed four months in which to transport our sacred possessions, including fifteen banners, from Sidi bel Abbes to Camp de la Demande near Aubagne in Provence. The Eternal Family will never die. I have a different occupation now, but what does it matter? You may be too young to be a Légionnaire, but with luck never too old.'

After accepting a cup of coffee our much-decorated friend did his best to persuade us to spend the night with him. He lived nearby. We assured him he was *très très gentil*, but alas, it was not possible. We still had far to go that evening.

'But *pourquoi? Pourquoi?*' he protested. When I told him, incautiously, that I had served in France, briefly, after Dunkirk, he seized my hand. 'But we have so much to discuss,' he said. I shook my head, sadly. At this he went back to his jeep and returned with a bottle of marc.

After more coffee and much more marc than we drank, the dedicated warrior told us he was on the brink of his seventieth birthday. Before the war he had served in the High Atlas from central Morocco to Tunisia. In May 1940, as a *Sergeant-Chef* under Colonel Monclar, his battalion captured Narvik and returned to France, and eventually Port Soudan via Brest. After battle honours in ill-fated Indo-China, his active service ended in Zaralda. His opinion of

Vichy was 'a government of folly'. As for *Le bon Charlie* (de Gaulle), he considered him an unapproachable man. He looked down on things. It would have been easier to be on intimate terms with the Eiffel Tower.

Before we said goodbye he reproached us again, gently, for being in such a hurry but admitted he felt a little unsteady. *'Je vous donnerai une phrase employée par mes anciens camarades dans les circonstances similaires: à moi les murs. La terre m'abandonne.'*

On the last stage of that seemingly endless day we mulled over fragments of what our friend had told us about the brigades in what he referred to affectionately as the Eternal Family. He said the ranks of the Foreign Legion, even their commanders had been drawn from over a dozen nationalities including many Germans and would-be Beau Gestes from Britain. Surely no other army in the history of the world could be compared with them? I thought of Alexander the Great, and of thirty Roman legions with their swarms of auxiliaries pressed into service from Spain to Pontica on the shores of the Black Sea, but had no wish to dispute with a proud and honourable soldier.

Little can be said about the appearance, the history and economic importance of Antikira since, after a shore-line walk, we arrived there at dusk and left before dawn. What's certain is that, with energy flagging, we found it a most hospitable place. All the action seemed to be centred on the tree-lined and lamp-lit square flanked by shops. Everyone had something to say to us. It didn't matter what they said, their nods, their smiles and chatter were of the very essence of goodwill. Compare this with crowded Oxford Street or the Strand, where you wouldn't get a squeak out of a stranger unless you happened to tread on his toes.

We sat on a bench outside a taverna, trying to give the

impression we weren't gulping down pots of Amstel. Within a few minutes up came a young good-looking fellow with curly red hair not often seen among Greeks. He was incongruously got up in bloodstained apron and laced-up cowboy boots. He held out his hand. 'Hiya, folks. Nice to see you. My name's Gus, Gorgeous Gus they called me in Chicago. Guess them damn Yanks in the stockyard couldn't pronounce Giorgios. That's my butcher's shop over there.'

We got the impression that Gus the Fixer just about ran Antikira, a town sung about by Homer and razed to the ground by troops under Philip of Macedon. To our surprise we were told this by Gus.

'Yeh! I used to have the job of acting as Greek interpreter at the British School of Archaeology in Athens. They was digging around here about twenty years ago. Somebody – guess it must have been a Brit, though I can't remember the guy's name – had found a temple where they worshipped Artemis. Pity the dig closed down when they ran out of money – they paid me ten bucks a day just for talking.'

That generous fellow the Fixer seemed put out that he couldn't fix anything for us. Not a good little hotel, his brother's place? Wouldn't cost us a dime, he said. Food? Anything except lamb. Every lamb from Patras to the Piraeus had been slaughtered for the May Day festivities.

He paused. He lifted up his forefinger and leaned forward confidentially. 'Say, what about a plate of fried mussels with a salad of black-eyed peas?' The very idea made our mouths water. Yes, we said. Would he have a drink?

He shook his head. 'Guess it'll take Ma Kassotis half an hour to fix something. I'll go have a word with her an' tell you when it's on the cloth.' He walked back to his shop. We heard the sound of a chopper on a block. He came out. He waved to us and walked off quickly, carrying a blood-stained parcel of meat. Barter is fairly common in small country towns.

And generous barter it was for one of the best meals we'd eaten in days. Ma Kassotis, his great-aunt, left us with a starter of *mezedes* – olives, almonds, shrimps and hard-boiled eggs – and then went off to cook the mussels. A blessing to find a Greek restaurant well stocked with a variety of fresh dishes after the eternal lamb stew and moussaka.

She came back with mussels, dipped in batter and fried in olive oil, and served with plates of sliced vegetables dabbled with garlic sauce. We ate rather too much, and there was more to come. She put on a local speciality, almond pears and nutty balls of icing which, with a nipperkin of mulberry liqueur, slid down like meringues.

After coffee Gus turned up with a short fat man and a distinctly shifty-looking fellow. He introduced them, chatted awhile and then dismissed them, summarily. 'Fatso', he said, 'likes to think he's mayor. It's his wife who tries to run the place. The other bastard is a *malakismenos rouphianies.*'

'A *what*?'

'A wanking pimp. Police informer. One of these days he's likely to get one between the eyes.'

Time to go. The bill came to little more than the equivalent of an English pound, which we reckoned hardly covered the cost of the wine. Useless to argue. Katie embraced Ma Kassotis. Gus kissed us both, told us where to sleep on the top of the hill, and said, 'May your hours be good ones.'

Without putting up the tent we unzipped our double sleeping-bag and slept apart, each in a private cocoon, each on a mattress of one of the fly-sheets cushioned by towels and spare clothing. I stretched out and gripped Katie's hand. Owls called. A shooting star drew a chalky line across the immensity of the night, and we were asleep within minutes.

Somewhere around three or four in the morning I woke up. To judge from Katie's contented and scarcely audible snores hordes of frustrated mosquitoes had turned on me. I had been bitten several times around the face, neck and arms. No amount of wriggling deeper into the sleeping bag afforded protection from further attacks, heralded by that fearful near-hypersonic whine. Remembering that my mattress, the inner fly, was equipped with a ventilation panel, I tried to pull it over my face. Wholly ineffectual – the gauze couldn't be comfortably arranged. Nor could I find the unused tube of insect repellent.

A bad night, that. I wriggled about and woke Katie, too late to act on her suggestion that we should put up the inner fly. At five o'clock we were brewing tea in that Tiepolo-blue light which is the mother of dawn.

On our way to Kirra at the foot of the Sacred Way I scratched like a dog. Despite antihistamine ointment my face and arms were pink and swollen. Katie hadn't been touched. Strange, this. We both thought we were relatively resistant to mosquitoes which, to breed, are given to gorge themselves with blood – Katie because, as the widow of a tea-planter, she had spent fifteen years in Ceylon. I had travelled extensively in Belgian Congo and the Canadian tundra, investigating supplies of that vital element, uranium.

All outside activities in Uranium City, a shack town of less than a thousand residents at the eastern end of Lake Athabasca, were strictly conditioned by 'skeeter hours'. Between six o'clock and half-past eight at night, and approximately two and half-past four in the morning, there arose a high-pitched hum, like a large dynamo heard at close quarters. It came from 'the slew', a mid-town pond which couldn't be drained as a spring sprung from a marsh some twenty feet below the surface. The fearful hum came from the wing-beats of billions of 'skeeters'.

Uranium citizens had more than their share of problems known to those obliged to live in the outbacks of North Saskatchewan and the Territories. High among them was what to do about the slew.

They could have used soluble pesticides, or oiled the surface heavily, which would have put paid to the skeeter larvae in a matter of hours but made for problems of public utilities in a community where tolerably fresh drinking-water cost over a dollar a barrel.

All this took place in 1953, when the outcome of the Korean War couldn't be foreseen – hence American interests in Canadian uranium. When I was there the slew had begun to stink, the skeeter problem had intensified, and the chances were that if it hadn't been for regular outbreaks of arson the water would have been drained at whatever cost.

As a radio and newspaper correspondent* on the look-out for feature material, I learnt from Kurt Larsen, owner of the Uranium City hotel, the only one in town, that their wooden shacks were being fired at the rate of one or two each week. To what end? 'Insurance,' he said. 'Everything in this town burns well and the volunteer fire brigade charges over the going rate for water.' He reckoned there was one man behind it working on a percentage basis, but apparently even the Mounties didn't know which one.

Those who should have known better than to be out and about in the bush during skeeter hours were hunters and prospectors, according to Doc McDougall who, Kurt told me, hadn't been cold sober for six years. Speaking with some authority, the Doc put it down to booze. 'If they

* BBC and the *New York Times*.

strike it rich the silly buggers are apt to get a skinful, leave their tents and wander into the bush in the hope of knocking off a deer.'

He said if they got lost without even the protection of smoke from wood fires they were at extreme risk, not only from dense clouds of skeeters but also from minute Black flies known to the Indians as No-see-ums. Men who got bushed had been known to tear their clothes off and, partly blinded, wade up to their chins in lakes. The Doc had seen their bloated bodies when they brought them in days later.

No-see-ums, he assured me, could kill Wood buffalo. Apparently most big game such as elk, caribou and moose were protected by thick fur, but Wood buffalo were only partly acclimatized to Jack pine scrub. They were refugees from their natural habitat, the declining forests of noble conifers on the edge of the Great Plains. Their genitals were almost naked, an easy source of an unprotected meal for Black flies. Agonized by ferocious attacks the buffaloes' last resort was to run their underparts against rocks which, if unduly sharp, occasionally lacerated them to the point where they bled to death.

With a room in Kurt's hotel for ten bucks a night I made more recordings there than I should have done with limited supplies of tape. On alternate Fridays when truckloads of miners from distant syndicates swarmed in with a fortnight's pay in their pockets they raised merry hell. They diced, played cards, sold skins behind the back of the Hudson Bay Company, argued and sang bawdy songs.

On those occasions Kurt hung up a notice which said in letters two inches high that anybody who hit a man would be barred for at least a month; those who took pot shots at bottles on the bar would be thrown out for the weekend and charged five times for the liquor spilt; but if anybody bust a window or one of his huge fly screens he wouldn't be seen there for at least a year. They took skeeters seriously in Uranium City.

'But why didn't they have a go at me last night?' asked Katie.

'Simple answer: I don't know. Maybe they're particular. Nothing but the best for a high-class Greek skeeter. Could be something to do with our blood groups. When I earned a living writing about science I remember a chap at the Tropical Institute studying malaria who reckoned that people in certain groups were more immune from different kinds of blood-sucking flies than others. There's also this business of skeeter hours. I can hear the damned things at a range of two or three yards but I didn't hear a single peep until they woke me up somewhere around three in the morning.'

She persisted. 'You say there's an ecological place in the world for everything, but what have skeeters got to offer except make an awful nuisance of themselves and breed more skeeters?'

I went on at some length about the inter-related web of life especially in the tundra where in many places there is about as much water as land. In the spring the Territories are invaded by millions of migratory birds, including at least a dozen species of flycatchers.

At this point I recalled the curious story of how a distinguished Greek, Professor George Mangakis, in a letter which he smuggled out of prison, described his affection for three mosquitoes. At that time, that is on our way to Kirra, I could recall only the bare outlines, but later I looked it up.

I would like to write about a friendship I formed the autumn before last. I think it has some significance. It

137

shows the solidarity that can be forged between unhappy creatures. I had been kept in solitary confinement
for four months. I hadn't seen a soul throughout that
period. Only uniforms – inquisitors and gaol keepers.
One day I noticed three mosquitoes in my cell. They
were struggling hard to resist the cold that was just
beginning. In the daytime they slept on the wall. At
night they would come buzzing over me.

In the beginning they exasperated me. But fortunately I soon understood. I too was struggling hard
to live through the cold spell. What were they asking
from me? Something unimportant. A drop of blood –
it would save them. I couldn't refuse. At nightfall I
would bare my arm and wait for them. After some days
they got used to me and they were no longer afraid.
They could come to me quite naturally, openly. This
trust is something I owe them. Thanks to them the
world was no longer merely an inquisition chamber.

Then one day I was transferred to another prison. I
never saw my mosquitoes again. This is how you are
deprived of the presence of your friends in the arbitrary
world of prisons. But you go on thinking of them,
often. *

John Berger, who reported the foregoing, commented that
animals were the first subjects in palaeolithic art, and the
blood of animals was perhaps the first paint used by Man.

The day, to put it mildly, had its ups and downs. Easy
stuff for the first few hours, all of it on a small but steep
road. Then down towards the village of Desphina where,
before we got there and after we'd turned our tired backs,
regretfully, on the *plateia*, the resort of serious drinkers, we

---

* *Second Nature*, edited by Richard Mabey, Cape, 1984.

stopped and considered in all their discriminatory pos-
sibilities the significance of three signposts. Experience had
taught us to distrust them. The first two, both modern
affairs, pointed due north to Delphi. The third, a worm-
eaten piece of old pine erected, we liked to think, before
Byron got there, showed some reluctance at disclosing in
Greek characters that, if the dirt track due west were
followed, travellers less sceptical than ourselves would reach
– distance unstated – the place we'd talked about for days:
Kirra. We took to it with no marked enthusiasm.

Although it couldn't be seen because of immense cliffs,
below us lay the Sacred Way. The marvel is that, historically,
it remained inviolate for so long.

Towards the end of the sixth century BC when Athens,
ever mindful of Persia, became a dominant sea-power,
Sparta, 'that city without walls lying low among the rifted
hills', broke the might of her Peloponnesian neighbours. All
her considerable powers were directed towards violent but
devious expansion. True Spartans were an élite; all lowly
work was carried out by serfs. Young Spartiales were selected
like favoured stallions and subjected to atrocious severities.
They were marched for hours on end, trained in weaponry,
flogged in initiation ceremonies until they fainted. They
were encouraged to fight each other, naked, in gangs until
the losers were physically laid low with broken limbs or
thumb-blinded eyes. No rigours ever matched those Spartan
battle courses.

Athenians, Thebans, Lydians, Scythians and Plataeans
sought Sparta's aid, but she always temporized when asked
for reinforcements. The moon was in the wrong quarter for
immediate action; her diviners proclaimed that birds of prey
had been seen flying against their interest. She could never
throw herself whole-heartedly into the affairs of greater
Hellas beyond her own doorstep. Elsewhere she probed,
delicately, like the tentacles of an octopus. And where better

than through the back door into Phokis with an enormous prize on the way; that is at Delphi where oracular supremacy was fortified by treasure for which we have no modern counterpart. Riotous indignation would break out against domination of the Sacred Way from Kirra to the shrine under the cleft of the Phaedriades. But there are back doors to your neighbour's allotment, and it seemed likely that we were on one of them.

The Sacred Way

Pausanias put it about that Homer referred to the very ancient port of Kirra as Krissa in both *The Iliad* and the *Hymn to Apollo* but Peter Levi won't have this. He says firmly that they were and are different places. Arriving at Kirra tired, hot and thirsty, we were totally underwhelmed by the information. All we wanted to know at that moment was whether the first taverna we came to served well-cooled Amstel.

A downright dull place on the lines of Peacehaven between Brighton and Beachy Head, a ribbon-developed strand of nondescript holiday homes. Few people about. No shops to speak of and nothing in the way of safe harbourage. Yet here it was, not long after Minoan times, that ships bearing merchandise and votive treasure inched their way through the western narrows. They were beached on what is now the Gulf of Itea, and a succession of invaders struck north through the gap between Parnassus and Giona into the rich plains of Boeotia and Thessaly. Here was the gateway into central Greece; herein lay the beginnings of Delphi, the navel of the classical world which for the centuries preceding the Persian Wars held a place comparable to the medieval papacy.

Itea today is the western extension of Kirra, indistinguishable from the old landing-place except that it's coming to life as a small modern port and bathing-resort instead of providing the last resting-place for a condemned fleet of rusting tankers. Hotels are springing up in the vicinity of the best restaurant within twenty miles, run by the brothers Stamatis. We ate, we slept, and when the sun poured over the peaks of Parnassus we began to climb up through an ocean of olives, one of the biggest groves in Greece.

Not the best time for tackling an unrelenting slope of six miles between the sea and the site of the oracle, except that the trees in that horticultural forest had been planted close to each other and with a little thought and much use of the compass we kept in the shade of their small, leathery grey-green leaves, silver below. They were sprinkled with greenish-white flowers which, Katie said, smelt of mignonette. She would have been of a different opinion in the last century when the ground was thickly manured with cast-off rags left to rot until the stench, it was said, could be detected by the crews of incoming ships.

Ancient agriculturists believed that the olive wouldn't do well if planted more than a few leagues from the sea. Theophrastus of Lesbos, that extraordinarily gifted if pedantic philosopher, put the limit at 300 stadia which is less than 40 miles. Simple observation shows that he was wrong, but the general principle is sound and the sea-misted crops north of Kirra are reckoned the finest in the country. Trees in good, that is to say calcareous, soils grow to a height of between twenty and thirty feet. They develop large twisted trunks covered with smooth grey bark which cracks into scales with age, and in the sun-dappled light we were fascinated by the remarkable variety of their branches. The general impression is one of angularity like the sketch of a tree by John Craxton or the winter silhouette of a horse-chestnut.

Olives attain a prodigious age. Some plantations are

supposed to have existed from the time of Pliny. From those trees above Kirra we looked for clues to the land-holdings and climatic history of Phokis. Could it be that some of the oldest, the stumpiest inhabitants with vast girths and a mere crown of greenery had been planted by Byzantine serfs in the days of the redoubtable Basil the Bulgar-slayer? What of those sawn-off limbs, all at the same height on trees of the same age on the edges of south-facing clearings? A winter of furious gales not long after the Turks arrived?

Here and there we saw well-defined groves of middle-aged trees which had been not so much pruned as carefully shaped by axe and saw. Had the owners inherited a property in disrepair, or was this the product of a pandemic of beetles, olive flies or fungus? Without constant vigilance, olive trees attract hosts of pests, invertebrate and botanical.

The unanswerable question is at which period prehistoric man began to cultivate the olive from what Virgil described as 'the unblessed wild plant with its bitter fruit'. In the Homeric world, as depicted in *The Iliad*, olive oil is known only as a luxury of the wealthy, an exotic product prized chiefly for its value in heroic toilet; warriors anointed themselves with it after the bath. Achilles sang sadly about how the body of his bosom friend Patroclus, slain at Troy, was sprinkled with the oil, but there is no mention of it among the foodstuffs of the heroes nor does it find a place on the Achillean shield which depicts the vine. However the presence of the tree in the garden of Alcinous who befriended the wandering Odysseus and carried him home in one of his magic ships shows it to have been not uncommon when *The Odyssey* was probably first sung.

All tradition points to the limestone hills of Attica as the place where it was first cultivated on the Hellenic peninsula. When Poseidon, Girdler of the Earth and Athena of the Flashing Eyes contended for the future city, the legend is that an olive sprang from the barren rock at the bidding of the goddess. That this legend has some association with the planting of the first olive in Greece seems fairly certain from a remarkable story told by Herodotus.

When the crops of the Epidaurians of Argolis on the Saronic Gulf withered away during a drought, the citizenry sought the advice of the Delphic oracle. They were enjoined to erect statues to those symbols of fertility, Damia and Auxesia, which had to be carved from the wood of the true garden olive, then possessed only by the Athenians. The request was granted on condition that they made annual sacrifice to their patron and founder, Athena. The command of the Pythia was thus obeyed and their lands again became fertile. The sacred trees of the goddess are said to have stood for long on the Acropolis and, though destroyed in the Persian invasion, they sprouted again from the roots and suckers when they were planted around the Academy.

We strode on, always upwards, always through those seemingly endless symbols of victory and peace until first, on a huge mound, we could see the little village of Krissa and then, high above it, the cliffs behind which, we knew, stood Delphi. Thereafter we struck a little to the east. The trees thinned and the ground became precipitous and strewn with boulders until we came to the almost dry bed of a torrent, the Pleistos which, in the season of melting snow, thunders down through a gorge immediately below the site of the Oracle.

There we sat on a spur of mica-glistening rock, drank strong local wine and munched bread, cold quail and chopped onions prepared by one of the brothers Stamatis: fare fit for an heroic landscape.

Far below we could make out Lilliputian ships heading for Itea on the Gulf. They were probably ferry-boats, colliers or the caiques of sardine-trawlers, but in our mind's eye they became full-bellied merchantmen sailing before the